Published by Dove and Orca, available from Bookmasters

at 800-247-6553 or www.amac.org (a great place to start

learning more about the autistic-spectrum disorders)

ISBN: 0-9668528-2-6

This book is dedicated to those parents of children with autism who carry through on programs, working their fingers to the bone to help their children build skills. Mary Pat Hartnett is a fine example of such a parent and has agreed to accept this honor on behalf of such parents all over the world.

This book is also dedicated to the memory of Michael Urbont, the great man, teacher and friend who first introduced me to psychology. Mike was one of the ultimate family men in the world. He would have wanted me to dedicate this to his family, so I will honor that wish.

Proceeds of this work benefit the programs of organizations working to better the lives of people with autism. The donations from this book and <u>When Everybody Cares</u> were inspired by Harry Chapin, who gave of himself before it was fashionable for celebrities to do so.

"Every year we make more money, every year we give more money away. Every December I have a meeting with my accountant. Each year he tells me the same thing: 'I've got good news and bad news. The good news is that you made more money than ever. The bad news is that you ain't keeping it!' But that's how it should be. . ." (paraphrased from Chapin's 2,000[th] anniversary concert at New York's Bottom Line).

Table of Contents

Foreword
Bobby Newman

In New York City, there is a special training called AMAP that enables one to hand out medications to students who have had medications prescribed for them. I arrived for training at the OMRDD office one Monday morning, prepared for the week-long training. The instructor asked us all to introduce ourselves and tell what we do. I introduced myself and explained that I was a psychologist at an agency for people with autistic-spectrum disorders. I was stunned when he promptly asked me to leave. I was getting kicked out of AMAP training! I felt like Rodney Dangerfield, not getting any respect. Maybe I should have used my preferred title, behavior analyst. Auguste Comte always said psychology was an immature discipline, anyway.

I asked why I had to leave. He informed me that his understanding of the regulations stated that AMAP training was only for direct care workers, not for supervisory personnel. I have to admit, my feelings were very hurt. Yes, I am a supervisor. I am also a direct care worker. Case in point: the bathrooms at AMAC were specially designed to accommodate my computer and printer so I can write programs while the child I'm toilet training is on break. To be honest, I get vomited on quite frequently. Either I'm a direct care worker, or I need to seriously reconsider my lifestyle.

That was one of the first things that really attracted me to

Applied Behavior Analysis (ABA): watching everyone work together in an egalitarian fashion. I'll admit it: I didn't always work and play well with others when I was young. I had a dose of arrogance a mile wide (now it's down to a half of a mile). The idea that you're only as good as your data really appealed to me. "You mean it doesn't matter what my degree is or how old I am, my voice is equal to the quality of my data and analysis? COUNT ME IN!" When I found out that behavior analysts generally avoided the use of statistics, then I was really sold. Another confession: I was no statistics student. I was the king of partial credit on exams and sacrificed two textbooks to the gods in my frustration at my inability to understand what was going on in stats class.

Now I'm in a supervisory role, and I transmit to trainees exactly what was transmitted to me: you're only as good as your data and intervention. Wave your fancy degrees and certifications at a self-injurious behavior. Huff and puff about how educated you are while trying to teach a child to speak. When you realize how useless your bluster is, you can get down to work.

This book is a sequel to my book, When Everybody Cares: Case Studies of ABA with People with Autism. This time around, though, I'm just the editor. I've contributed a few chapters, but the bulk of it is written by friends and co-workers. They vary in job and degree from school psychologist to parent to speech therapist to teacher assistant, but they all have something in common: they are direct care workers. They don't shout encouragement or give orders from an office a mile away. They're in the classroom, doing their thing. Bottom line: if a professional doesn't get his or her hands sticky from primary reinforcers or get sweaty from playing with the children, don't trust the person. They're not worthy of the title "professional." What's more, they're not worthy of the much more honorable title, "direct care worker."

It may sound like a cliche, but direct care workers are the real backbone of ABA. This is not a platitude, this is solid fact. There are too many students for the Ph.D.'s to see each one individually. Even if we could see that many individual students, generalization is what we really need to work on. Only by having a great many people involved in the effort can we hope to effect real, long-lasting change. A professional may give the program the push, but it's the direct care workers who keep it going, and their input that steers direction.

I'm really proud of this work, and the people who have contributed. Many are former students or trainees, and all are great to work with. More importantly, all have distinguished themselves by their dedication, skill, and intelligence. It is the goal of any good teacher that one day his students will be better than he ever was. I don't think I have much to worry about.

Chapter One: The Student is Always Right
Dana Reinecke

"Do this," the teacher said, tapping her knees. I watched proudly as my young student tapped her own knees. This was the child that had screamed for the entire duration of our first three sessions. She refused to make eye contact. She could not talk. She did not play. She challenged the physical endurance of some of the strongest men I knew by running away from them, wrestling with them, crawling under tables and hanging on to the table leg when they lifted the table to find her. Within one month, she was able to sit with a teacher, attend, and begin to imitate.

I started working with Jenny when she was just 2 years old. She was one of the most beautiful children I had ever seen, but her deficits were so severe that I felt a little daunted by the prospect of working with her. Her avoidance behavior was so extreme that I felt compelled to warn her mother each time I worked with Jenny that she might scream and cry, and that I could not be interrupted, no matter how bad it got. Jenny was lucky enough to have a set of parents who not only loved her and wanted the best for her, but were strong enough to make difficult choices for her. They let me let her cry, and by the fourth session she didn't cry anymore. Within three months, she was starting to talk. Within a year, she could speak in full sentences. Within 3 years, she was in a preschool for typically developing children.

She now has so many friends that her mother had to go back to work to pay for all the birthday presents they have to buy; Jenny is at a party every weekend.

But that's not the point of the story. The point is, when her school district sent a teacher over to provide some of the many hours of discrete-trial teaching Jenny was getting at home, I went to meet with the teacher, observe her work with Jenny, and explain some of the programs we were working on. When that teacher said, "Do this," and tapped her knees, and Jenny tapped her own knees, the pleasure that I felt in seeing Jenny succeed was quickly replaced by a sinking feeling. The teacher had taken a raisin and popped it in Jenny's mouth, saying loudly, "Good girl!"

I knew what was coming. Sure enough, Jenny's eyes grew wide, her lips moved into an indignant pout, and she began to scream.

I would get upset, too, if someone threw food into my mouth.

Putting edible reinforcers into a student's mouth is one of my pet peeves. Nothing looks worse, or takes away independence and dignity more, not to mention the fact that many students just don't like it, and the food quickly loses its reinforcing value.

Jenny did not like having food put into her mouth. In fact, she didn't like other people touching her food. Who can blame her? At the time, I worked with at least 3 children a day, smoked, ate, drove, pumped gas, handled money. I washed my hands frequently, of course, but I shouldn't have been touching anyone else's food anyway. I'm sure that Jenny didn't know what the rest of my day consisted of or the danger of germs, but I respected her feelings anyway. When we were using edible reinforcers, I would offer her the plate and she would daintily pick up one piece of food and put it into her own mouth. Jenny and I liked our relationship and sessions to be as civilized as possible.

That experience taught me a valuable lesson. It was something I always knew and respected, but hadn't verbalized yet. The fact is, the student is always right. Whatever he or she is *History* doing at any given time is a function of his or her environment. When behavior increases as a function of a stimulus being contingent on that behavior, that stimulus is a reinforcer, whether or not we think it should be a reinforcer. Just as importantly, when behavior is *not* increasing, the stimulus that we are presenting is *not* a reinforcer. *an Rt is not an Rt (Premack)*

What I find even more interesting than these basic truths of behavior is that sometimes it is not *what* the reinforcer is, but *how* *only if you don't believe* we give it that makes it reinforcing. In Jenny's case, food was a reinforcer only if she could pick it up and put it into her mouth herself. That's actually pretty terrific, especially for a two-year old child with a severe disability. Edible reinforcers may be socially inappropriate, but if a child can and prefers to feed herself, it's just a little less inappropriate.

I worked with another child who preferred to take his own reinforcers. His name was Manny, and he was a student in a preschool where I consulted for a few years. Manny was one of the first students that I encountered at the preschool and one of the main reasons that I was contracted to provide consultation. The teachers described him as "out of control" and "unmanageable." They nearly began to twitch when they talked about him. I was, I admit, skeptical about how "unmanageable" a three-year-old could be. Of course, even a small child can engage in severe problem behavior, but a child that age should be relatively easy to physically prompt, or even carry or restrain if necessary. When I met him, I felt even more smug that I had walked into a piece-of-cake job. He was tiny, blond, blue-eyed, and could have been a model for one of the cherubs in the Sistine Chapel.

Then I sat down with him. He screamed, kicked me, bit me, smashed his head into the wall behind him. An hour of blood, sweat, and tears (literally) later, we had accomplished nothing. I thought about the reinforcers. After consulting with his teachers and observing Manny, I had a selection of toys that Manny played with frequently. These were things he chose himself, and would be engaged with for hours. Yet, whenever I handed him a toy, he would resume screaming, kicking, etc., and throw the toy as hard as he could across the room. Slowly, it began to click. If he chose it himself, Manny would play with a toy. If I handed it to him, he threw it. Chose . . . play . . . get . . . throw.

The next time I sat down with Manny, I placed his favorite

toys on the table next to us. As soon as he was sitting quietly, I said, "Great sitting!" and got up and walked away. The teachers looked at me like I was crazy, but Manny just turned to the table and began to play. When I approached him again, I gently took the toys away and again reinforced good sitting by allowing him access to the toys. Gradually, I began to build in a more stringent definition of good sitting, and I was able to introduce some simple instructions. Within a few days, Manny was working on his programs, making progress, and engaging in no disruptive behavior whatsoever. When we graphed the data, we saw that he cried, screamed, was self-injurious, and/or aggressive during 100% of 10-seconds intervals prior to allowing him to choose his reinforcer. When Manny was given the opportunity to choose his reinforcer, the problem behavior decreased to 0% of the intervals and stayed that way.

Just as in Jenny's case, the stimulus was the same, but the method of delivery determined if it would be a reinforcer or not. Both Manny and Jenny liked choosing and taking their own reinforcers, even though there was no qualitative effect on the actual reinforcer itself. I have speculated about why these children responded to the opportunity to choose their reinforcers the way they did. Perhaps in Jenny's case, the anticipation of having the food in her hand was just as enjoyable as eating it. Perhaps for Manny, other people just couldn't give him the right toy at the right time, and giving him the opportunity to choose from a selection meant that he always got just what he wanted most.

It really doesn't matter, though, why reinforcement took this form for these children. What matters is that it did, and that the people in their world who were working to teach them recognized it and conformed the program to their particular learning styles. ABA is not a set of tricks; it is a set of principles, which means that it is always applied on an individualized basis. We must always remember to do what works for the child, as long as it is not dangerous or socially inappropriate. In fact, sometimes our students may surprise us by wanting more independence than we realize they are ready for, like Manny and Jenny.

Chapter Two: An E-mail from a Parent
Josephine Parent

(Note from the editors: this is an e-mail that one of our contributors received from a parent of a child with an autistic-spectrum diagnosis. This parent had been contacted to thank her for giving an obviously impromptu speech at a meeting, following a parent who had gone off on a rather destructive tangent. The contributor had related frustration with the fact that he had heard about some of ABA's best people actually being threatened with lawsuits when children did not "recover," as well as the failure of several parents to carry through on crucial treatment plans to encourage more age-appropriate and independent behavior that would make their children more able to make it in mainstream settings. Understandably, the parent has chosen to publish this chapter under a pseudonym.)

"Hi name. I haven't stopped thinking about our conversation all day. I am so disturbed to hear of what people in the ABA community are having to deal with. There are so few people out there that truly understand autism and give of themselves so unselfishly in order to make positive and lasting changes in children and families like mine. I hate the thought of professionals and/or the science being "blamed" for anything and I cringe at the thought of good, ethical and dedicated practitioners having to defend themselves (if even given a chance to do so) in such public forums as internet chat rooms and dysfunctional "support" meetings. I have often been frustrated over how much time parents spend complaining. If you exchanged the complaining time for productive teaching interaction time with their kids, they'd have far less to complain about.

Name, I have only known you for a short while but I have known "of" you for many years. From a parent's vantage point there is one word, although I could add many others, that fits you best and that word is 'caring.' It breaks my heart to know of your tremendous frustration.   I wish I could offer some advice but instead I can only offer a request - or rather - a plea. Please keep doing what you're doing on behalf of all of us, and keep training others to do so. We need your willingness, your experience, your commitment and your wisdom.

I wish I could offer an answer to the field's problems - I can't. As you well know, parents are learners too. Each is motivated and reinforced by different things and each has their own set of variables contributing to their behavior. Just like with the kids, there is no "cookie cutter" Rx to help parents "get it" and to get them to comply and follow through on things they are asked to do. I think a major problem is that most never really get enough consistent practice or direct supervision to allow them to become skilled or proficient in modifying their children's behavior. They never gain instructional control, they don't witness any significant changes, and therefore they are not motivated to keep at it. Instead you hear "it's not working."

I used to tell the behavior analyst overseeing my son's programs that it's like losing weight. If you've ever tried to do it (I've spent my whole life working at it) you know that the first 10 pounds are the most difficult. Once those pounds are shed, you see "observable and measurable" changes, i.e., pants are looser, clothes look better, you feel better, etc. At that point , the positive changes that are occurring are so heavily reinforcing that the "dieting" behavior is easily maintained. But . . . . for the person who never gets to the 10 pound mark - the one that struggles with the same 5-10 pounds for years - they never get to the point where the positive changes are obvious, and therefore dieting remains punishing instead of reinforcing. I don't know if that analogy is the best one to describe the difficulty in getting parents to follow through, but it is the one that comes to mind first.

It's funny - I was not scheduled to speak at the meeting, but felt compelled to do so in an effort to "smooth over" some rough spots that you obviously noted and in an attempt to add some credibility to who we were and what we were trying to accomplish. But that's a whole other story . . . . . . "

Chapter Three: The Recovery of Teddy
Adrienne Robek

When I first met Teddy, I didn't even know where to begin when it came to working with him. It was the first time I had really worked with someone with autism. I can still remember the dread I felt when my supervisor told me I would be working in his classroom. I was hoping for a group of sweet, cuddly, and most of all, easygoing preschoolers. This four-year-old boy was a force to be reckoned with. It's amazing how such an adorable little boy can wreak such havoc.

Teddy was our number one tantrummer. He tantrummed on the way to the bathroom, on the way to the classroom, during circle time, during discrete trials, if it was raining, if it was sunny, if it was 12:00 on a Tuesday, you get the point. It didn't help matters that Teddy was not only big for his age, but he had this extraordinary talent of being able to twist his body in such a way that no matter how hard you tried, you just could not hold him in his seat. Working with him was a lot like having a workout at the gym.

Teddy loved to use the element of surprise when battling it out with the staff. The swift kick to the shin, slap across the face, and head butt came to be his trademarks. At times, he would even become self-injurious by slamming his head into the wall, floor, furniture, etc. There were times when I would seriously contemplate getting out of this field of work. I would wonder if I was really cut out for it. No matter how much I struggled with him, I just could not get his behaviors under control.

It was obvious that Teddy had a lot of potential. He was very aware of his surroundings and on the rare occasions that he would sit and attend during discrete trials, his scores were phenomenal. For all the battle scars he gave me, I still kept at it. I knew there was so much more to Teddy than he was letting everyone see. The only problem was that at that point I didn't have the experience I needed to help him in the best way possible. I tried working with him exclusively for a few days, hoping to show him that no matter what he dished out, he could not beat me. It didn't work. About five months after he first walked through the classroom door, we decided to try something new. It was so simple and required so little effort in comparison to what we had been doing that we were skeptical that it would work. A new consultant suggested that we try something called "planned ignoring." As Teddy seemed to find attention very reinforcing, we just wouldn't give him any while he was being non-compliant.

The first day was absolute chaos. Teddy was non-compliant and the behavior was ignored. Although his behavior was being ignored, he was not allowed to just wander around the room and do as he pleased. The classroom had four small work areas that contained few or no distractions. Teddy had to stay in his work area while his behavior was being ignored so we could make sure that he was not engaging in any reinforcing activities. *No - past history* He couldn't understand why we weren't giving him attention and would begin to tantrum. This is what is called an "extinction burst." He was having a burst of inappropriate behaviors in the hopes that we would all come running to him and give him what he wanted. First he would scream, hit, cry, kick, spit, and most of all, throw various objects around the room. Still, he was given no attention for this misbehavior. Teddy was not allowed to participate in any reinforcing group activities until he had completed all of his programs for the day. We were using lunchtime with the other children (as opposed to eating by himself), gym, art, and circle time as reinforcers for compliance. Along with these activity reinforcers, Teddy was given a reinforcer of his choice that could be earned and consumed during discrete trial work.

The second day of our planned ignoring program brought with it an entirely new element. As none of Teddy's inappropriate behaviors were getting him the attention he so desperately wanted, he decided to take a new approach. Teddy began urinating in his pants. Mind you, Teddy was fully toilet trained at this time and had been for quite a while. I guess desperate times call for desperate measures. He apparently thought we would all come running to change him and finally give him some attention. It didn't work out exactly as he planned. He knew where his change of clothes was and if he wanted to change into clean clothes, he would just have to do it on his own.

After a couple of days, Teddy's tantrumming decreased. His non-compliance, however, took a little while longer to get under control. Just because he wasn't having a full-blown tantrum didn't necessarily mean he was doing all of his work. The scenario went something like this: a staff member would sit down at a table in one of the work areas with Teddy and attempt to do discrete trials with him. We would ask him to do something (e.g., touch his head), and more than likely he would refuse. He would go about doing this in one or a combination of ways. These methods included blatantly ignoring the request being presented by the teacher, turning his head away from us, closing his eyes, and/or falling off his chair and lying face down on the floor. Even throughout all of this, we were beginning to notice a few subtle changes in Teddy. He was gradually getting more of his programs finished, rather than playing dead. Before we started our planned ignoring treatment program, it was taking Teddy, on average, about three to four months to master a program. After we were able to get his behaviors in the classroom under control, he began mastering programs at a much faster rate. It was only taking about one month on average to master each program.

Unfortunately, we were still having problems with Teddy's tantrums during transition periods. If we were going from the classroom to the bathroom or vice versa, for example, we could expect a tantrum. As the planned ignoring wasn't working as well with transition as it was during discrete trials, we decided to take a different approach. Every time Teddy went to the bathroom and back to the classroom without being non-compliant, he was given a piece of chocolate. Chocolate was a very strong reinforcer for Teddy and, to make sure it stayed potent, we used it only to reinforce appropriate transitions. At no other time during the day was he given chocolate.

After a while, an amazing thing happened. Teddy began to talk. Up until this point, Teddy was using PECS (Picture Exchange Communication System) to communicate. Of course, in the beginning, his articulation was far from perfect. It was, however, an accomplishment for all of us (especially Teddy). In the beginning, we were using PECS to supplement his speech because it was very difficult to understand what he was trying to tell us. Soon, however, we were able to understand most of what he said and took him off the PECS. He now loves to talk. He speaks spontaneously and has a lot to talk about. He is always going over to staff and telling them all about the book he is looking at or the toy he is playing with. He has also taken it upon himself to tell on the other children when he sees them behaving inappropriately. It might sound like he is "being a brat," but this is something that many typically developing four year old children do as well.

Teddy has developed an amazing ability to generalize the skills taught to him in his programs. An example of this is how he generalized a program that taught him how to perform novel actions with different toys. Instead of always doing the same three or four actions we taught him with the toys, he is now able to play in novel ways. He plays appropriately with every toy he is given, most of which were never used in his programs. He is now able to learn new material incidentally and in groups. Even though his speech is not perfect, and he still perseverates once in a while, he is a completely different person than he was when I first started working with him. This dramatic change took about eight months to complete. Recently, Teddy went for a psychological evaluation and lost his diagnosis of autism. He still has severe language delays and the occasional tantrum, but if the next eight months are as successful as the past eight months have been, there's no telling what Teddy can accomplish. It's strange to think that the reason I almost left this field is the same reason I decided to stay with it after all.

Chapter Four: From Tears to Laughter
Tami Lavie

In November of last year, three year old Sharon attended a newly opened class at the preschool where I am employed. Sharon entered my classroom with tears in her eyes, and cried throughout the rest of the day. There were a few games on the tables, and Sharon took three puzzle pieces and went to a corner of the classroom behind a cabinet. Every time one of the staff members approached Sharon, she would scream and cry. But, in spite her crying, we had her participate in all the activities.

The next morning, Sharon entered the classroom crying, and again took the same puzzle pieces. When it was time to work with her, I took her and sat on a chair in front of her. She cried and avoided my attempts to make eye contact. I felt that it was important that I get Sharon to trust me before I started working with her on regular programs (e.g., motor imitation, action commands and eye contact). This would make working with her more successful. I struggled to build that relationship.

I asked Sharon for the puzzle pieces, and she just ignored my request. I then took them and said, "This is giving me the puzzle pieces." Sharon cried again, and tried to get up from the chair. I then started to sing the song "Twinkle, Twinkle, Little Star," while forming a diamond shape with my fingers. Sharon did not look at me. She tantrummed in her chair, but I continued to sing.

As soon as I finished, I gave her back the puzzle pieces. She calmed down for a second, and I then asked for them again. Sharon reacted as she had before.

I did this 14 times. The fifth time, Sharon stopped crying as I sang the song. By the eight time, Sharon was holding both of my thumbs and making eye contact with me as I sang. Amazingly, by the eleventh time, Sharon gave me the puzzle pieces when I requested them. I felt that I had made some kind of connection with her, and that she was starting to trust me.

For the two months that followed, Sharon cried throughout most of every day. She would throw a tantrum every time she had to participate in any activity. She didn't eat, and cried at almost every meal, but we didn't let her go to her corner. She sat with all the children at circle time, crying and throwing tantrums. We decided to ignore her tantrums, however, and still had her participate in all of the activities.

Some of the children tried to interact with Sharon, but she just pushed them away. We designed several programs to work on with her. When we worked with Sharon, she did not follow any verbal directions, and therefore we had to do very long massed trials. We persisted until she did what we asked her to do. At first, we let her hold the puzzle pieces in her hands most of the day, as we saw that it helped her to calm down. We then used the pieces as reinforcers while doing programs with Sharon. To add extra "routine," each time we began to work, we sang "Twinkle, Twinkle,

Little Star" to have her acknowledge and trust us.

Sharon was not verbal, so we started working on the Picture Exchange Communication System (PECS) with her. Sharon did very well. She understood the concept of exchanging an icon for a desired object. Sharon did not make any progress in her other programs, however, as she continued to cry and tantrum throughout most of the day. After a while, we decided to change the way we had been doing programs with her. Instead of giving her an instruction and waiting for her response, we decided to employ a hand over hand prompting procedure. We sat with her, provided the instruction "Do this" (while clapping our hands) and then took her hands, clapped and said, "Good doing this." We then gave her a reinforcer. We followed this procedure for more than a month. We tried fading to hand over wrist, but Sharon did not understand the concept of performing the action to earn the reinforcer. We continued this procedure until, one day, after receiving the instruction, Sharon lifted her hands to get us to clap her hands. We were very happy, as this was the first time she showed any sign that she understood what we were looking for. The same thing happened with the rest of the programs. In color identification, for example, we worked on matching colors. We used two blue cards and Sharon had to match them in isolation. In the beginning, we did hand over hand prompting, but as soon as Sharon understood the concept, she placed the card in the correct place independently.

At the same time, Sharon gradually stopped crying. She started following the routine of taking her picture and putting it with the rest of the children's pictures on the wall during circle time. At snack and lunchtime, she sat down without crying, and most of the time we didn't have to physically prompt her to sit. Slowly, she began eating her snack. She still did not eat her lunch, however.

In programs, Sharon progressed very nicely in PECS, and slowly stopped crying. Once we saw that she understood the routine, we changed the trials to 9 times hand over hand, and the last time she had to do it by herself. In the beginning, Sharon tantrummed when she had to follow the instruction by herself. We had massed trials that lasted for 30 to 40 minutes. But, as time passed, she started doing them herself. Once she mastered this step (90% and above correct across two different trainers and three sessions), we changed the procedure to eight times hand over hand and twice she had to do it by herself. Sharon mastered this step quite quickly and then we moved to the standard way that we do programs with all the children (generally 10 trials for each program).

We followed the same procedure (hand over hand) with all of Sharon's programs. We worked with her on the following skills: motor imitation, action commands, body part ID, color ID, eye contact, directed play, PECS, and labeling objects receptively.

Sharon's behavior changed rapidly. I remember that her parents used to write in her communication book that she smiled at home. We almost did not believe them. We never saw Sharon smile, and it was almost impossible to imagine her doing that. But, of course, they were right. After three months, Sharon smiled for the first time in school. It was so amazing! We were in the movement room, a place where the children get to run around, play with balls, and work on their gross motor skills. Every day, Sharon would tantrum the entire 30 minutes we were there. We did not let her take her toys to the movement room, so she would try to open the door and go back to the classroom. Gradually, Sharon stopped crying in the movement room, but it was almost impossible to engage her in any group activity. One day, while we were in the movement room, Sharon was walking around the room. Suddenly, we realized that she was smiling. Even though she was smiling to herself, we were thrilled to see that she was happy.

We noticed that Sharon also smiled in the classroom. She would smile to herself when she was in her corner with her toys, but, after a while, she smiled at us as well. We have circle time twice a day. The children sit in a half circle facing me. When I call each child by name, they get up, move their picture from one place to the another on the wall, sit on my lap, and then we all sing group participation songs. During the first few months that Sharon was in the classroom, she would cry and throw her body on the floor whenever it was her turn to move her picture and sit on my lap. I used to do hand over hand prompting while taking the picture, and then sit her on my lap and sing the songs. Sharon screamed and tantrummed, but I never gave in. Finally, after about two months, she stopped crying and one day she even smiled while sitting on my lap.

Sharon exhibited the same behavior wherever we went. Twice a week, we go to the computer room for about half an hour. Sharon didn't like the computer room and used to tantrum every time we went there. We used her toys as reinforcers whenever she sat. She was not interested in the computer screen, but we wanted her to stay in the room with the rest of the class. More or less by the time Sharon stopped crying in the classroom, she stopped crying in the computer room.

One day, we found out that Sharon could laugh. It was a few minutes before it was time for the children to go home for the day. Sharon was sitting on my lap, while I was singing to her. Suddenly, she made eye contact with me and smiled. I then gently blew in her face. Sharon started laughing and she looked so happy! I did it again, and it was just amazing. She was laughing hysterically. I called the other staff over to see Sharon laughing. They would never have believed me if they hadn't seen it for themselves. From that day forward, Sharon laughed a lot. We found out that she likes tickles and being lifted up in the air. Every time she wanted us to do one of these things, she would look at us and reach her hands toward us. Now, we are having her vocalize as well.

Today, Sharon is a different child compared to when she came to the school. In programs, Sharon is making observable progress. She follows one-step directions and her eye contact is much better. She imitates a few hand movements and matches 10 colors. Her behavior is great; most of the day she smiles and runs to us for hugs and kisses. At times, she holds my face, looks into my eyes and kisses me. While working, Sharon rarely tantrums anymore, although sometimes she tries to avoid a task by hugging us. During snack and lunchtime, Sharon sits nicely and eats her food. Sharon is a very smart girl; she has progressed amazingly over the past year. Other workers at school who used to hear her cry and scream all day have trouble believing that this is the same girl.

I think that the main reason for the change in Sharon's behavior was our persistence. We never gave in to her tantrums; we worked with her, and had her participate in all of the activities, despite her tantrums. We believed in Sharon and knew that one day she would stop crying and start laughing. Her parents report that at home they see the changes every day. Now, every time Sharon wants something she points to it and vocalizes instead of crying as she had before.

I would like to take the opportunity to thank all the staff members who worked with Sharon and taught her to smile and be a happy and a loving girl. Thank you Elana, Sinead, Michelle, Sharla and Susan.

I would also like to express my appreciation to Sharon's parents, who work with her day and night and come to the school to learn how to work with Sharon. They follow every suggestion we give them and the work they are doing with Sharon is inspiring and effective.

(Note from Bobby Newman: Following the completion of this chapter, Tami came to me one afternoon. "Sharon can talk," she excitedly announced. Tami directed me into the elevator, where Sharon was preparing to go home for the day. Tami then gestured to Sharon's book-bag and labeled it. Sharon then repeated the label, clear as day. The imitated labels have since given way to formal requests. Sharon has begun to request many items within the classroom, and the culmination came this past week. Her dad asked her if she wanted Mickey Mouse, when in fact it was a Minnie Mouse that he was holding. Sharon looked up at her dad and very clearly corrected him: "Minnie!")

Chapter Five: Utilizing Written Prompts and Teaching "Out of Order" for a Child with Autism to Learn

Laura M. Pajot

During my first year as an ABA teacher, I ran discrete trials "by the book." I was taught that first the child must acquire the receptive portion of the skill, and when (s)he demonstrates comprehension of that skill (and verbal ability), the expressive component may then be introduced. I was extremely interested and passionate about this work, and, being slightly obsessive, I strove to be perfect. For the better part of my first year, I did what I was taught, fearful that if I deviated, I would "contaminate" the child, and cause problems with his or her learning.

In September, while teaching my first ABA class, I met a child named John. John was four years old, recently diagnosed as Autistic, and demonstrated many of the typical characteristics of Autism. Some examples of these characteristics were delayed and immediate echolalia, tensing, flapping, pacing , an affinity for printed material, and an affinity for letters and numbers.   Armed with this information, along with his past test scores and professional reports, I set out to create a "program book" designed for John, based on my training and knowledge.

John's program book contained many of the early pre-readiness programs that you would expect. Responding to name, gross motor imitation, receptive commands, and receptive object identification were just a few of his programs. As the year went on, John progressed slowly but steadily in the areas of imitation, receptive commands, eye contact, and self-help skills. Receptive object identification was going nowhere fast, however.

It was now June, John was being moved to another classroom, and I began working with him at home. Over the course of the next year, his progress slowed. I was trying everything, so I thought, to get him to begin to identify objects. We began using preferred toys, dolls, etc. . . but to no avail. His progress was inconsistent, at best.

At this point, John's classroom teacher and I were becoming very frustrated. One day I realized, however, that he could independently label all the picture cards that we were using for verbal imitation. I immediately changed his entire program. It appeared that he was going to learn the expressive component first, utilizing pictures!!! We would then use the picture as the prompt over the full verbal cue, to elicit the response that we were looking for.

This approach appeared to work for a while, and John was able to label many pictures. The problem that we were now facing was that he could not request items in real life that he had learned in session. We moved to utilizing his knowledge of the pictures as a prompt to generalize the skill to all objects.

It also became apparent that he acquired labels more quickly when they were paired with a written prompt. Again, his program was revamped, and a program called Object Identification was begun. This was not your typical discrete trial approach to object identification. What we did was take one room of the house at a time, and label everything in the room, along with providing various representations for each object in picture form. We started by going into the room, and while pointing to the object and its written label, began running this drill as we had run the verbal imitation program mentioned earlier. Within a few weeks, he began to label the object, as well as the pictures. At present, we are planning to teach every room in the house in this manner, as his progress in this program is the quickest I have seen yet. We will fade out the written label, and believe that he will eventually retain the object label, as well as the picture label.

Perhaps the most interesting, as well as functional, use of written prompts comes in the form of a sentence board. Last summer, I was sitting with a colleague of mine and we were brainstorming for a way to teach John to begin to utilize the object labels, as well as request items spontaneously. Up until that point, his requesting had been very inconsistent, and it appeared that retrieval of words was very difficult for him.

I wanted to use the most successful method to teach him to request items. Although I felt that a PECS system would be successful, it would not be functional for this family at this time. What I did instead was write up very small functional phrases, laminated them, put velcro on them and made my sentence board.

First, I trained up five sentences in the same format as the verbal imitation program mentioned earlier. Once he was able to recognize the sentence and independently read it aloud, the sentence was placed into a functional teaching phase. We would have the board out at all times. Whenever the situation arose, be it natural or artificial, we would use a gestural prompt (pointing) to the appropriate phrase so that John would use it appropriately. For example, a favorite reinforcer of his was tickling. Two of the trained up phrases were "do it again" and "tickle me." We would tickle John and then abruptly stop. He would grab for our hand to resume tickling him. We would then bring his hand to the phrase on the board and he would read it aloud. As a result, we would resume tickling him.

The sentence board has proven to be one of the most effective tools in John's programming thus far. Currently, he is up to about twenty phrases, and has been successfully generalizing many of these to his environment **without the presence of the sentence board**! We will continue teaching John phrases in this manner, and eventually develop a more sophisticated sentence board that will deal with all facets of his life.

When Bobby asked me to contribute a chapter to his next book, I knew fairly quickly what I was going to write about. I have been working with John for almost four years now and have learned so much from working with him. I think the most important thing I have learned is that ABA and/or discrete trial teaching requires an extremely high level of creativity, as every child learns differently. I have also learned that there really are "no rules" when trying to get a child to learn. If (s)he can't learn the receptive component first, try the expressive component. If objects aren't working, try pictures. If neither are working and the child has an affinity for letters, try utilizing written prompts. Basically, what I'm saying is, try it all!!! Whatever works is the "correct" way of teaching. Just make sure that there is a component built in for generalization of the learned material into functional everyday life. Otherwise, what's the point?

Chapter Six: Linda's Silence is Broken
Sharon Toledo

Several years ago, a four year old girl walked into my classroom with her mother. She stood, holding her mother's leg and refusing to let go. Her mother informed me that Linda was very shy and that she could not talk. I bent down to Linda and waited for her to peek out at me. I greeted her and extended my hand. She hid again. Her mom, Margaret, began to tell me all the reasons behind her shyness, and the most heavily emphasized reason was her inability to talk. Margaret explained that Linda often got upset when she wanted something or needed to tell her mother something. Margaret wished Linda could at least say "mom." A few days later, Linda and I began our quest!

A program was developed which incorporated Linda's strengths (attending and motor imitation skills) and addressed her weaknesses (communication skills). Linda was able to sit in a chair and make eye contact. On occasion, however, she needed to be prompted to look. Her communication deficits were severe and I hoped that her motor imitation skills would generalize to imitation of sounds. It was not quite that simple!

After several days, I evaluated Linda's progress in the area of verbal imitation. She was not saying "mom." She was, however, vocalizing "ahhh." This was frustrating Linda because she was not receiving any reinforcement during her verbal

41

imitation trials. Something had to be changed. I did not want the verbal trials to become aversive. I had to make reinforcement attainable during those sessions. I decided to use a shaping procedure whereby Linda would begin with what she could say ("ahhh") and gradually shape her sounds closer and closer to the target word, "mom." Linda responding with 100% accuracy during these trials, with no recorded "frustration" behavior. It was time to move the program to the next level.

Linda was now required to roll her lips inward, as if attempting to verbally imitate the sound "mmm." At first, I had to physically prompt her lips to close by rolling them inward with my two fingers. She found this to be very funny and attempted to do the same to me. This behavior was only permitted for a very short time (approximately 3-4 sessions). I did not want to discourage this social behavior, but it could interfere with our work. After one month, Linda was able to roll her lips with 80% accuracy across three therapists. Again it was time to move closer to the target sound of "mmm."

This was the hardest part. I was able to manipulate her physically from the outside, but how could I prompt sounds from inside her mouth? I began by asking her to say "ahhh" and then attempt to close her mouth on the sound as she was saying it. After two months, she was able to do this exercise on her own. I now had the job of preventing her from physically manipulating her own lips. This was frustrating for her. I distracted her by telling her to "help me" make the sound with my lips. We did this together for several sessions, mostly through her tears. She mastered this "mmm" sound after another 2 and a half months. Linda was now ready to put these two sounds together to make her first word.

I began the session with some pre-trial 2-step motor imitations (roll lips closed and open mouth round). She responded with 100% accuracy. Linda was then told, "say ma." She had difficulty in the beginning. She was confusing the placement of the two sounds. She would say "mmmmmm-aaaaahhhhh" and then "aaaaahhhhh-mmmmmm." The two sounds were separated by a pause. The pause was eventually eliminated with practice. I began to play with these two sounds with her. I would start with "mmm" followed by "aahh" followed by "mmm." She began to imitate the sequence. After 6 months, on a hot August day just after her 5th birthday, Linda called her mom into the room with a perfect "MOM!" Margaret was thrilled and told us that it was worth the wait.

Today, Linda is 6 years old and attends an ABA classroom in a public school. I still work with her at home 2-3 times a week. As a final note on the matter, Linda recently called 2 very special behavior analysts on the phone to tell them that she missed them . . . yes, she is talking more every day.

Chapter Seven: Finding a Communication System for Jay
Amy Eisenberg

One of the biggest barriers faced when teaching children with autism is their difficulty in learning speech and language skills. Past studies have shown that only 50% of children with autism ever develop speech for the purposes of communication. These same studies, however, also state that the vast majority of children with autism end up in institutions. As anyone working with the autistic population knows, these percentages are becoming increasing outdated due to intensive and effective early behavioral intervention.

Communication is arguably the most difficult, yet crucial, skill for children with autism to learn on their journey into a mainstream society. Perhaps I am a bit biased because of my background in speech and language, but my claim is supportable. Every living organism needs to communicate at some level for survival. Communication is essential, even if the children might not realize it yet. If one cannot communicate via verbalizations/speech, (s)he must find other ways in which to get needs met. Although children with autism can be quite creative and resourceful in getting their needs met without intervention, their resources may also be quite limited. Initially, to obtain desired items, their repertoires may not involve much reciprocal interaction. Their repertoires usually consist of great physical dexterity (e.g., climbing or opening items that seem to defy their ability and strength) or hand leading (using an adult's hand as an extension of their own body). When their needs are not met, however, they may try to communicate/request via screams, cries, or they may even become physically aggressive towards others and/or towards themselves. Keeping in mind that we always want to use the least restrictive treatment model, we first attempt to increase appropriate communication (verbal or non-verbal, depending on the child), as this will decrease the number of inappropriate behaviors (e.g., aggression) we need to deal with. In this manner, the focus of intervention remains a reinforcing experience. It is for this reason that I argue that communication is one of the most crucial skills for a child with autism.

Okay, enough said about the philosophy. Now about Jay (a fictitious name, but one that I adore because it is that of my husband). A quick background history: Jay was developing normally until about 18 months of age, when abruptly his language skills and most of his social skills came to a halt. In October, at 2 years of age, he was diagnosed by a pediatric neurologist with Pervasive Developmental Disorder (PDD). By March, Jay had begun 20 hours a week of intensive in-home ABA therapy. When he began programming, Jay was virtually non-verbal. The only true word in his vocabulary was "bye." He was enrolled in an early intervention school where he was being taught some sign language in order to communicate. He showed little success with this system. Once in-home programming began, it was decided after assessing Jay's lack of communicative progress with signs and his strong visual skills, to try another augmentative communication system, PECS (Picture Exchange Communication System). PECS has an advantage over signing in that it uses easily understood picture images. Unfortunately, most people in our society do not understand sign language.

As hypothesized, Jay quickly learned the early phases of programming, which taught Jay to use a picture to request or comment. As the program advanced into distinguishing between icons to request, however, Jay began to have difficulty. After meetings between team members, as well as the team's behavioral consultant and representative consultants from Pyramid Education, Inc. (who were extremely helpful), we tried numerous modifications. These modifications consisted of additional prompts given before and during the production of a communicative response. In behavioral terms, these are called response and stimulus prompts. Some of the response prompts included modeling and physical guidance. The stimulus prompts included varying the proximity of the icon in reference to the actual object, pairing the icon with the actual object, varying the size of the icon, having borders versus no borders, and even using real pictures (created from a CD, Picture This) and actual labels of the items. At this time, however, the icons were becoming highly aversive to Jay, so much so that even the sight of them caused aberrant behaviors.

We then decided, as a team, to temporarily augment the PECS system by using an augmentative communication device which was both visually (lights up when button is pushed) and auditorially (speaks the label of the item requested) stimulating. It was a large, electronic device that required Jay to push one of a few large, clearly separated rectangular buttons before receiving the desired item indicated on that button. Initially, an isolated, highly desired item was paired with the PECS icon on the button. Jay would reach for the desired item and we would physically prompt his hand down to first press the button. The small light would then come on and the device would simultaneously play the recording of the desired label. With that, Jay's request was reinforced with the desired item.

Initially, Jay enjoyed using the device. We systematically decreased the proximity between the actual item and the icon so that Jay would need to focus on the picture representation of the item and not just the item. We also systematically added more icons. When he met criteria for one icon, we moved to two, and eventually to three items. At three items, we again encountered difficulty in meeting criteria. Jay was having trouble associating the picture with the object for the purpose of requesting. This difficulty appeared to be only with requesting. In other programs, Jay enjoyed matching. In fact, Jay almost flawlessly would rapidly match any object to its picture, even when the picture wasn't exact. Communication using the device was again becoming highly aversive to Jay, so we decided to put the pictures on hold (for communication purposes). At this time, Jay was approximately eight months into therapy. He would sporadically use whole words, and at times, even a short phrase appropriately. It was highly inconsistent, however, across people, place, and time, and no pattern appeared to emerge. He was excelling in all imitation programs, gross and fine motor tasks, and visual problem-solving tasks such as puzzles. We were also beginning non-verbal and oral-motor imitation programs.

At this time, for communication, we were requiring precise pointing (not hand-leading) towards the item or object he desired. Upon his pointing, we would slowly move the item towards our eyes (prompting Jay to visually track the item to make eye contact). Once eye contact was established, we simply stated the item name (e.g., "sprinkle") and he immediately received the reinforcer (the sprinkle). Although this may seem like a long interval between Jay's request by pointing and the receiving of the item, the whole exchange was done within 2-5 seconds, depending on tracking time.

All of the behavior therapists and Jay enjoyed this program. It seemed to facilitate more reciprocal communication between Jay and the rest of the world. The pointing gave him a way to communicate with the world, and he happily embraced this new manner of communication. As Jay continued to thrive in his programs (with the exception of auditory language processing, i.e., following directives), his aggressive/aberrant behaviors showed a significant decline. Therapy was becoming more pleasing to him. His greetings towards me went from cries and "bye" (Jay's former nickname for me, i.e., Me: "Hi, Jay," Jay: "bye") to an occasional smile and virtually no crying.

When Jay reached mastery criteria for requesting via pointing, we of course had to up the ante to vocalizations! As before, he had to point to items. Then, upon hearing the object name, he had to attempt a vocal approximation of the word. At this point, any sound was acceptable, with the exception of a cry or a whine, as objectively defined by our team. Jay was doing well with oral motor imitation programs. Additionally, as his non-verbal imitation skills improved, his spontaneous vocalizations and jargon were simultaneously increasing. Slowly, but systematically, Jay was showing an increase in his use of vocalizations to request. We began to shape his vocalizations into verbal approximations.

It was now March, our one year anniversary with Jay. He had gone from basic programming, such as appropriate sitting and eye contact, to play programs including pairing the action with verbalizations (e.g., in doctor play, say "ahhh"). Nursery school songs went from "Row, Row, Row Your Boat" which required Jay only to hold hands and move back and forth to songs such as "The Wheels on the Bus," pairing words with appropriate gestures. The cutest part of the song was "the mommies on the bus." He

49

would crinkle his forehead and purse his lips, extremely tightly, with his little finger over them and say "sh, sh, sh" all three times, as required by the song. Therapy was becoming a lot of fun for everyone. Jay knew he was understanding and showed such excitement and pride in himself! His parents would tell us, almost daily, about some skill he had generalized, either with them or in school.

Within two weeks of this verbalization spurt, Jay's processing showed remarkable improvements. After a year of trying to randomize various one-step directives, on March 15, 2000, Jay followed the randomized instructions "throw it away" and "tap table" with 100% accuracy! In fact, it was easy for him. It appeared that after a year of utilizing various strategies to help increase his receptive (comprehension) and expressive language, something finally "clicked." Not only did it click in one area, but across many. It appeared that all of the skills were somehow connected, which we had speculated all along.

To improve his language skills, we had to incorporate many prerequisite skills including fine and gross motor. By working with the whole child, we were able to teach him very specific skills. When speaking about Jay's success, I don't mean to mislead anyone that it was all smooth sailing from there on. We have had minor setbacks and I'm sure the future will bring more, but even on the most challenging days, Jay's behaviors are not as uncontrollable or as long in duration as they were in the past.

Learning is a continuous process, and we will continue to analyze what is currently working best, or not working, in teaching Jay and modify our approaches as needed. One thing for certain is that Jay is definitely on his way to a much fuller and more enriching life in mainstream society because of early and intensive behavioral intervention. I am not claiming that it was only the behavioral intervention that helped Jay, but behavioral intervention is the only treatment that is systematic and proves the existence of a functional relationship between therapy and a child's responses/behaviors.

In retrospect, there appeared to be three key elements to Jay's success:

1.	To truly believe that Jay, as well as all children, are capable of learning. Since the beginning, we all knew that Jay had the capability of learning. We were just not sure to what extent he would reach his personal best. We still do not know. As Catherine Maurice once said at a conference at Queens College, "with your children, always reach for the stars but accept the clouds."

2.	Active engagement: a child is not going to communicate if there is no need to communicate. We must constantly assess the child's progress in order to alter the treatment if it is not being effective in creating skills that are reinforcing to that *individual* child. Again, communication must be rewarding for that child if we expect him or her to want to communicate.

3.   The third key to our success was looking at the entire child. To work on speech and language, you can just work on speech and language goals. We worked on all domains: cognitive, social, fine and gross motor, ADL skills, and speech and language. Without pre-requisite skills such as proper motor control for sitting and pointing/grasping, or social skills for waiting, and eye contact or cognitive skills for auditory and visual discrimination, how can one begin to address "traditional" speech and language goals?

Additionally, and perhaps most importantly, was the coordination and participation of everyone in Jay's life in his meaningful social environment.

Many parents believe that if their child has deficits in speech and language, the more speech and language therapy, the better. More, however, is not always better. Of course, I believe that a child can benefit from "traditional" speech and language services, but a child with such severe deficits also needs help in many domains, not just speech and language. Additionally, a qualified speech-language therapist can be valuable not only to the individual child, but can serve as a valuable resource to any program, center-based or in-home. A speech-language therapist can effectively train others to incorporate speech and language therapy goals into all programs, interactions, and environments.

Chapter Eight: For the Love of ABC's
Odeisa Hichez

When I started to work as a teacher for children with autism, I realized that the major challenge of this job was to communicate with the children. With most of the children unable to speak or otherwise express their needs, how could I know why they cried or tantrummed, when something hurt, or when they needed something? At first, I felt that my only option was to guess, until I got to know the children well enough to know their habits and routines. Nevertheless, it was a great surprise to see that, although many children with autism were not able to speak, they could either hum or sing a song. What a puzzle! During my first two and one half years work with children with autism, I observed that many of them loved music. I always sang to please them, without really appreciating the powerful communication tool I had on my hands. . . until I met Martha.

Martha was a nonverbal, 4 year old girl with autism. She was not toilet trained, displayed very poor eye contact, and had a short attention span. In addition, she seemed emotionally unstable, frantically laughing at one moment and bursting into tears the next. Due to her inability to communicate effectively in any age-appropriate way, she would become very aggressive and destructive. Martha cried desperately, scratched, kicked, hit the staff and other children, and threw everything in her way when she was unable to express her needs or have them met.

Martha was unable to engage in any kind of interaction. Her gross motor skills, such as running, climbing, jumping, crawling, and hopping were within a normal range for a child her age. Martha loved legos and puzzles, which she mastered just a few minutes after playing with them.

After being in the school for about four months, Martha was still not able to master any of the communication techniques we tried to teach her. Then, we noticed that Martha loved songs. She was very attentive whenever somebody was singing, especially during circle time. We were even more amazed when we first heard her humming circle-time songs like "The ABC's," "Old McDonald," "The Wheels on the Bus," "If You're Happy and You Know it," or the transition songs we sing while we move around the school. Her favorite song was the ABC's. It took her a while, but eventually she was able to hum the entire song.

At school, Martha's Individualized Education Plan (IEP) goals were met through Applied Behavior Analysis (ABA), on a 1-to-1 basis. Included among her discrete trial teaching programs was verbal imitation, the first step being to get her to imitate the sound "P." Martha became very frustrated when working on this specific step, and usually ended up having a tantrum due to her inability to comply with the request. At those moments, I felt discouraged too, knowing that although she could hum the whole alphabet, I could not get her to articulate a single letter.

One day, it occurred to me to sing the ABC's song as the prompt for Martha's verbal imitation program. I sang the complete song over and over again to get her attention. As she loved the song, she happily paid attention to me. After several trials, I would stop at the letter "O," hoping for Martha to continue the song for me and say "P." In the beginning, she became really distressed, throwing tantrums every time I stopped the song. We went on like that for quite some time.

I started to feel hopeless about getting anything from Martha through the ABC's song when, one day when I least expected it, she finally just got it. I was astonished and filled with joy at that moment. That was nothing, however, compared with the big smile and ecstacy I saw on Martha's face when she finally articulated the sound. It was just fantastic and so rewarding, after trying so hard.

Initially, Martha did not respond consistently. Sometimes, she would say "P," but other times she would cry and get upset again. I kept working on it, until she consistently complied by completing the song with the letter "P." Once she mastered the verbal imitation with the song, I started to work with the prompt, "Martha, say 'P'." It was a "piece of cake" for her after this. Even better, she began to receptively and expressively identify the letter whenever I showed it to her, either in isolation or with distracting stimuli. Once this was achieved, I worked on generalizing her response to other contexts.

I then initiated working with other letters: A, B, C, and so forth until Martha verbally imitated the entire alphabet. Once more, with the mastering of the verbal imitation of the rest of the alphabet, it became possible for her to receptively and expressively identify all the letters.

This was a major breakthrough for Martha, as well as for the staff working with her. Not only did she verbally imitate us and expressively identify the letters of the alphabet, but she also began imitating words and then phrases. By the end of the school year, Martha's repertoire included,

> "bathroom,"
>
> "hi name,"
>
> "bye name,"
>
> "tie shoes,"
>
> "want cracker,"
>
> "want cookie,"
>
> "want water," and
>
> "want toy."

All of these phrases were spoken independently and spontaneously whenever she needed to use them.

As Martha became able to speak and communicate with the staff, her aggressive behavior decreased significantly. Her functioning in the classroom really improved, as well as her comprehension skills. She also became a lot more compliant in everyday activities like arts and crafts, playing, and other ABA discrete trial teaching programs we were trying to teach her. Of course, Martha was now able not only to hum her favorite songs, but to sing them as well.

My experience with Martha made me realize how powerful music can be. I never thought it would be possible to get a child with autism to learn to speak through an ABC's song. I often see the wonders of music in my work, however. Many children who were otherwise non-verbal became able to sing, and even more importantly, socialize with their peers. It has been suggested that music offers a secure environment in which they can establish a contact (Alvin, 1976). The best thing about it is that you don't have to be Frank Sinatra to sing a song to a child. I have come to believe that not only might the child like the song, but also in that singing for them, as we put our own social insecurities aside, show our true selves and become a confident friend to the child.

In my classroom, the children liked the songs so much that otherwise non-social children voluntarily move over to circle time to sing in the group. At first, I see shyness and fear in their faces, showing that they are aware that they are being watched. As the other children and staff sing, this fades away. Perhaps music gives children with autism and developmental disabilities the opportunity to express themselves through the singing of words and phrases, making them aware of themselves and others, and thus promotes independent functioning (Boxil, 1985).

It is frustrating for the parents of children with autism and other forms of developmental disability not to be able to communicate with their children. It is even more frustrating, however, for the child not to be able to express his/her needs. There is a lot that can be done with a simple song. Every word sung is practice in manipulating lips, tongue, and oral musculature. While all children are unique, and certainly not all children with autism will respond to this prompting approach, let's remember that children with autism are still children. They like the same songs we liked when we were their age. They become happy when singing them, or even better, having somebody sing the songs for them when they cannot do it by themselves.

I have worked with children with autism in a preschool for more than 3 years now. It is a very challenging and rewarding job. The most important thing is to be patient, caring, and never give up on a child. Martha taught me not only the value of a simple song, but also that what you might least expect would be effective can lead to miracles. Often, when I am dealing with a child that is having a rough time or being frustrated by not being able to comply or communicate, I try singing during our down time. At that moment, a big smile comes to the child's face. One comes to mine too, as I look back and think about Martha and all she achieved just for the love of ABC's.

Chapter Nine: Physical Therapy and Occupational Therapy in an ABA Environment
Randi Scheiner and Deborah Kochman

I, Randi, am an occupational therapist (OT). I, Deborah, am a physical therapist (PT). We work with children diagnosed with autistic spectrum disorders, learning disabilities, and emotional disturbances (ages 3-12). This is nothing so unusual. What makes us a little different is that we are integrated members of an ABA-based school. We want to share with you the ways in which we have successfully utilized our skills as an OT and PT to promote our students' growth in their roles as children, family members, students, playmates, friends, community members and playful, independent explorers of their environments. It is our intention that you as caregivers for children with autism gain a clearer understanding of our contributions to the teaching of children with autism, and to identify and seek out occupational therapists and physical therapists as viable, integrated members of your children's ABA teams.

Physical therapists and occupational therapists are often associated with orthopedic/sports medicine, geriatrics, cardiac rehabilitation, stroke/brain injury rehabilitation, spinal cord injuries, and multiple physical disabilities. We are not as commonly associated with treating children with autism in ABA settings. Nonetheless, in any setting, physical therapists address a person's strength, tone, joint range of motion, balance, coordination, and motor planning. Occupational therapists help people maximize the above mentioned skills to increase their independent performance of activities of daily living. We teach children the skills they need in order to "be children" and to grow into adults who need minimum supervision. These skills include play and socialization (sharing, turn-taking, asking relevant questions), self-care (dressing, feeding, washing, grooming, etc.), academics (attending to classroom lectures, copying from a chalkboard, task completion), and community living (money and time management, etc.). Additionally, both disciplines emphasize cognitive development through therapeutic activities, and the management of sensory information (many children with autism get easily over-stimulated in what might not be overwhelming circumstances for typically developing people). We are quite at home within ABA schools for children with autism, provided the appropriate data-based teaching stance is shared by all.

A central point is that our training has equipped us with a special knowledge to help guide ABA interventions. It is important to appreciate each child as a unique social being, affected by and affecting the complex interaction of his or her motor, sensory, perceptual, cognitive, and social-emotional systems. We must carefully consider the entirety of a child's ever-changing environment as we apply ABA interventions. For example, when a child demonstrates oppositional or avoidance behaviors upon presentation of an activity, the source of his or her behaviors can erroneously be attributed to "laziness" or "being difficult" and this can confound a practitioner. With our training, however, we may observe poor muscle tone, poor balance, gravitational insecurity, overstimulating physical environment, tactile defensiveness, poor coordination, or lack of previous exposure to the activity. We assess all of these aspects, and more, to decide which factors prevent a child's full participation in a given activity. We then use specialized therapeutic activities to remedy deficits, enabling a child to participate in a full range of activities, and thus decreasing a child's oppositional or avoidance behaviors. Our unique diagnostic perspective helps us to make suggestions about WHAT needs to be worked on, as well as contributing to the HOW. Even the most powerful techniques, applied to the wrong problem, will not ameliorate the difficulty (See Table I for a list of factors evaluated by physical and occupational therapists).

While writing this chapter, several points became clear:

1.   First, contrary to rumor, ABA does not preclude the development of a warm, strong clinician-child rapport. This rapport is best achieved by learning about a child from a broad perspective, exploring the relationship between a child's behavior and his or her motor, sensory, perceptual, cognitive, and social-emotional abilities.

2.   Children often acquire new skills more easily when they are allowed to make choices as to the direction of sessions (i.e.,

choosing preferred activities as a reinforcer or deciding the order of the programs). We help develop the realization in children that they CAN maximize their existing abilities to learn new skills. We help instill self-confidence and a sense of skill mastery in children by providing them with opportunities for success, alternated with increasingly challenging tasks.

3.   In keeping with the basic ABA maxim, all human action can be considered behavior. Rehabilitation therapists are equipped with a variety of evaluation and treatment skills to teach functional behaviors. Our training in task analysis, for example, helps us develop and modify ABA programs in the motor skills and self-care domains.

4.   We can train staff to carry out necessary interventions within our specialty areas.

5.   We can perform the formalized evaluations necessary to initiate service delivery and diagnose difficulties.

6.   We are a valuable resource for treatment activity ideas for educators and parents of our students.

7.   Most basically, just as there is no "cure" yet for autism, training in ABA alone may not impart to clinicians all the knowledge necessary to design all interventions. Therefore, it is beneficial to access professionals with a variety of knowledge bases. When specialized knowledge is required, it is crucial to utilize specialists, such as physical and occupational therapists. They can supply the "what" to work on, even to the expert in

"how."

Before we relate the specifics of our work, let us attempt to clear up any misconception about the compatibility of related service staff and ABA, as we are aware that some ABA schools do not employ related service providers. In truth, there is no reason that related service providers cannot be fully integrated members of the ABA team. It may take time for the related service provider to learn to work on unfamiliar programs. It is also an adjustment to begin working within the completely empirical format, avoiding techniques that are not as completely data-based. Yet, for the reasons described above and below, we think it is an important investment in time and mutual training. We have learned behavior management techniques and the process of recording our sessions in quantitative, as well as qualitative terms. We have come to appreciate the relationship between ABA programs such as making eye contact and social greetings, and a child's acquisition of more advanced skills, such as making grocery store purchases, attending to a classroom lesson, or playing a board game with a group of children.

In the spirit of "all for one and one for all," we collaborate with speech therapists, psychologists, teachers, social workers, behavior analysts, and parents, and train staff to carry out empirically-based procedures. Deborah may notice tight heel cords in a child who toe walks, and recommend stretching exercises for the child to carry through with in class, gym, and at home.   Randi may recommend that a child's teacher set up a slant board and encourage the child to assume a more functional sitting position for a child with difficulty printing within an allotted space. As noted above, when necessary, we train staff to carry out the necessary interventions. This facilitates generalization and maintenance of student performance and thus increases student autonomy. The standard for practice at AMAC is that at any given moment, it should be impossible to know who is who within a classroom. A staff member we have trained may be carrying out a PT/OT intervention with a student, just as we might.

Let's consider a typical functional task. When teaching a child to identify and use a fork, a teacher, speech therapist and behavior analyst work together to create receptive and expressive discrete trial programs. As the child learns to identify a fork, the physical and occupational therapists teach the child how to hold and use the fork, maintain a comfortable and functional sitting position, and carry the fork from a counter to a table.   In conjunction with classroom instruction, we teach the parents to carry out our plans at home.

A hallmark of the OT and PT professions is the attempt to use treatment activities that are motivating to, and functional for, our clients and students. For example, we use board games to teach manual dexterity, finger strengthening, appropriate digital grips, and eye-hand coordination. We arrange hopscotch, hide and seek, bicycle riding, bowling, obstacle courses and hula-hoop games to teach balance, coordination, and praxis (motor planning and execution of a task). Art and cooking projects such as paper mache, finger painting, leather lacing, or making pudding are used to develop task focus, task sequencing, task completion, and a variety of motor and perceptual skills. The treatment activities we offer hold opportunities for children to exercise their creative self-expression, social skills, playfulness, initiative and independent exploration of their environments. We find that when carefully prepared and supervised, our activities help children develop their self-confidence, which in turn gives them the impetus to attempt more challenging academic and motor tasks. When we teach children functional skills, we can help decrease self-abusive and other non-productive behaviors.

As integrated members of the team, we develop and modify programs with attention to the specific functioning levels and needs of each child (see Table II for examples of such programs). Because of the emphasis on play, this teaching time is looked upon as a reward unto itself by many students, and this helps to develop functional skills. Our students often request to "earn" time with us, and we "sneak in" fun play activities that frequently generalize to the home environment. An enjoyable activity such as opening up a jar filled with toys helps a child develop the upper extremity strength and disc grasp to open a food jar at home.

Although we use play activities as a form of treatment, we do not abandon the data-based decision-making model. We are constantly collecting qualitative and quantitative data to assess the most effective therapeutic approaches. For example, we record how long a child holds a quadruped position while rolling a bowling ball and the extent and type (verbal, physical, visual) of cues needed to use a tip-to-tip pinch to pick up mini checkers.

Moving away from the STRICTLY empirical, we must remember that our students are people first. Along with the rest of the staff, we often help facilitate children's spiritual growth. We must not forget that the attention provided helps children feel more "human," cared about, and understood in an otherwise harsh and confusing world. This attention gives our students the confidence to try new and more challenging activities, which can lead to increased peer acceptance and praise from influential adults. This increased peer and adult acceptance and praise help shape a child's positive self-concept.

We conclude with a sample of skill deficits common among our children and treatment ideas to help children grow as functional, happy, socialized members of their families and communities (see Table III).

Table I
Skills evaluated by physical/occupational therapists

MOTOR
Mobility
Strength
Muscle tone
Range of motion
Reflexes
Force and timing of movements
Balance
Coordination
Endurance
Finger dexterity
Grasps and pinches
In-hand manipulation
Visual perception
Proprioception
Kinesthesia

SENSORY
Modulation of sensory input
Body scheme

SOCIAL-EMOTIONAL
Belief in personal effectiveness
Frustration management
Interests, habits, cultural values
Family dynamics and roles
Communication
Classroom skills

COGNITION
Alertness
Motor planning and praxis
Learning disabilities
Conceptual integration
Attention
Memory
Problem solving
Safety awareness

SELF-CARE
Dressing
Feeding/Oral motor
Grooming
Washing

ADVANCED DAILY LIVING AND COMMUNITY LIVING SKILLS
Money management
Time management
Personal space management
Social reciprocity
Pre-vocational skills

Table II
Examples of programs developed by occupational
and physical therapists

Physical Therapy Programs
Gross motor skill development using action commands
Gross motor reciprocal movement using imitation
Gross motor reciprocal movement and strengthening
Task Analysis: Transitioning from standing to sitting on the floor
Task Analysis: Transitioning from sitting on the floor to standing
Shoulder stabilization and strengthening
Ball-catching
Underhand throwing

Occupational Therapy Programs
Hand-washing
Dressing fasteners: buttons, snaps, zippers
Shoelace-tying
Belt-threading and buckling
Spreading butter onto bread
Utensil use
Toothbrushing
Printing/Tracing: shapes, letters, names, sentences, paragraphs
Scissor use
Pencil grip
Hairbrushing/combing

Table III
Sample skill deficits and treatments

SKILL DEFICIT	SAMPLE TREATMENT GOAL	TREATMENT SKILL COMPONENTS AND SAMPLE ACTIVITIES
Decreased self-care skills: zippering/unzipping a jacket/vest	Child will independently zip/unzip jacket/vest while wearing garment	Zippering program Finger prehension activities Bilateral coordination Eye/hand coordination Practice on bookbag, use zipper pull
Decreased graphomotor skills	Child will print first and last name within ½ inch lines using appropriate letter sizing and spacing	Tracing/printing program Trace over highlighter Stencils Chalk mazes on the chalkboard Placing yarn on pathway Eye/hand coordination games Use of visual cues (lines, stickers, and dashes) Vary writing implements Visual/spatial planning
Decreased lower extremity strength	Child will ride bike with training wheels independently for 10 feet	Squats Leg lifts sitting and lying down Marching in place and forward Jumping in place and forward
Decreased upper extremity strength	Child will walk wheelbarrow style for 20 feet	Wall pushups Modified push ups Pushing large ball with both hands and each hand individually

69

Chapter Ten: Verbal Imitation: A Break from Traditional Therapy
Scott Campbell

There are many traditional approaches to addressing deficits in speech production. Typically, preschool children with articulation problems can learn from structured play activities where target sounds are modeled and produced with increased frequency, known as auditory bombardment. If there is a motor component to the articulation deficits, then oral-motor exercises, such as blowing bubbles or making faces, can be utilized to increase strength and/or control.

At 4-5 years of age, a child should be able to produce most speech sounds or make a reasonable and consistent approximation of each sound. Typically developing children acquire these sounds through interaction with adult and peer models as they develop. Children with autistic spectrum disorders typically have barriers to learning, such as poor eye contact and isolation from social interaction. As a result, decreased life experience further hinders acquisition of speech sounds. A compounding problem is the incidence of motor speech difficulties which co-occur with autistic spectrum disorders. Such children may have a repertoire of sounds that mirrors that of a typically developing child, or can be limited to mostly vowel sounds with a few consonantal sounds in more severe cases. This was the case with Jason.

Jason was a 4 year-old boy who was not developing any meaningful speech sounds. He was neither progressing with his use of PECS (Picture Exchange Communication System), nor achieving mastery on most of his other programs. The isolated successes he had in discrete trials were in matching, sorting, and motor imitation programs. All of these required little if any understanding of the commands given to him and contained enough context cues that he could perform these without any verbal command.

Verbal imitation was first introduced as a formalized program in late October 1999, beginning with a sound that was already in his repertoire, "eh." In late December 1999, this step was discontinued due to lack of progress. All but two of the scores recorded in this program were massed trials, meaning that the trials were continued until a correct response was elicited. The two non-zero scores were 10% and 20%, which occurred randomly during this two month period. In collaboration with the behavior analyst on staff, a modified verbal imitation program was created and implemented on February 7, 2000. An approximation to be used for the new verbal imitation program was selected from sounds that Jason made with moderate frequency in his babbling. The consonant-vowel combination "bi" (pronounced "bee") was noted to be particularly frequent, and if needed, could be associated with a picture of a bee to assist in its production. Staff were instructed to model the "bi" sound as many times as necessary to elicit an imitation from Jason. Staff were to count how many models were provided before a correct sound production on Jason's part, and to take data on number of models. This is in contrast to a + for successful production and a - for an inaccurate production, as is typical with standard verbal imitation programs (i.e., we changed from percent correct to latency to imitation).

Jason's performance was as we had anticipated. It took 157 models to elicit the sound on the first attempt, then 127 on the second. It was decided then that only one trial of this program would be possible because of time constraints and the amount of focus taken away from his other programs. As a speech pathologist, I ran the program with more frequency than the other staff, who voiced frustration about the program and were not motivated to run it as often. Any time this program was initiated, staff and I expected to be face to face with Jason for as long as 45 minutes with our lips numb from our exaggerated models of the "bee" approximation. The greatest number of models provided before correct production was 285. Interspersed within trials of 200+ models were two instances in which only 15 and 31 models were required. In the first 4 weeks there was no discernable trend, however, that could be seen in the graphs of his scores. The lower scores of 15 and 31 were interpreted as nothing more than Jason playing with his bilabial sounds more frequently on that day over another day when he would be relatively silent or choose a guttural "kuh" sound.

Then, something exciting began to happen. No score over 200 was recorded after March 13th, approximately 5 weeks after initiation of the program. I was still skeptical, but hopeful that the technique was working. Only 4 times after April 6th was a score recorded that was over 100, but all of those were immediately following a 10 day spring break. I couldn't believe his progress, though it did not always feel like progress, especially when providing the 88th model of "bee."

Finally, on May 16th, it can be stated with the support of hard data that Jason gained the skill to consistently repeat a sound following only one model!! The new behavior was consistent and intentional!! By May 19th, he had mastered the "bi" sound and moved on to the next sound in the program. (Mastery criteria was that he imitated correctly on 90% or more of trials, across at least two teachers) The biggest fears we had came out in a flood. Would Jason lose this sound if we moved on to a new sound? Would he lose the sound over a long weekend away from school and discrete trials? Would he be able to produce only this one sound in imitation?

After many joyful tears from staff for the newly acquired skill and sharing our fears with each other, we were pleasantly surprised to find that his ability to imitate was not limited to the sound we had in effect "trained," but responding generalized, and he was able to imitate with a gross approximation of many consonant + vowel and vowel + consonant combinations. Some isolated success was even demonstrated with some two-syllable words, like "apple," which he produced perfectly.

Jason also began to focus his attention on the lips of the speaker and make better eye contact. A new feeling of connectedness was the most striking thing reported by those who knew him. Jason began to acquire new sounds rapidly. He continued to study the lips of the speaker, make approximations of words modeled for him, and to interact with staff and peers in a more meaningful way than ever before, with appropriate eye contact and attention.

Following his mastery of the first sound in his imitation program, Jason started to demonstrate signs of progress on his other programs as well. PECS was now being used in a book with 5 pages and multiple pictures on each page. Jason was even able to use a sentence strip with "I want" and the picture of the item he desired in place. Jason's number identification had typically been taking 2-3 months for mastery, and as of May 12th, each step took only 3-5 days to master. The first step in his eye contact program was begun in January 2000, and was mastered on May 25th. The two remaining steps took one week each to master. This is just a sampling of the effect that the ability to imitate can have on other programs, proving itself as a foundation for other skills.

Our technique was unique in the way that it did not focus on imitation at the beginning, but rather reinforced an already present behavior/vocalization to increase the probability of re-occurrence. Initially, reinforcement was delivered upon free-operant, or unelicited, behavior. As Jason became more aware of the stimulus given and the response needed to earn the reinforcer, he was able to learn how to imitate.

This example with Jason is an example of how the collaboration between behavior analyst and speech-language pathologist can be most valuable in treating speech and language deficits seen in children with autistic-spectrum disorders. A behavior analyst is knowledgeable about shaping behavior, and a speech pathologist is knowledgeable in speech and language development and disorders of speech. Each can benefit from the other's training in effectively treating these children.

This technique took a long time before it proved to be effective and, in retrospect, could have been implemented more efficiently. If the program had been performed with more frequency and by all the staff every day, the time it took for Jason to master the first step might have been shortened significantly. Since the staff of the preschool had never used this technique prior to working with Jason, and the anticipated effectiveness of the program was questionable, increasing the frequency of this program was not possible at the time. With the benefit of hindsight, I will not hesitate to aggressively use this technique with any children who have similar deficits as Jason. It is worth all of the frustration and the numb lips to give someone the ability to imitate speech, with all of the associated skills that verbal imitation can help develop.

Chapter Eleven: The Consistency Compromise
Heathyr Sheehan

It was one of my first experiences, working with what started out as a 7:1+2 (7 students, 1 teacher, and 2 teacher's assistants) classroom. It was all moving along smoothly, until Lucy came along. She completed the scheduled eighth student slot, and quickly filled the role as my "pet" in the class. The attraction about Lucy was that she was a funny kid, and she seemed to know it. Any seven year old who can laugh at her own jokes is a friend of mine, and a good one at that. She was an entertainer, a lovable child, and we shared some childhood interests in common. These included activities such as climbing on furniture, consuming all foods not nailed down (although I drew the line at the damp deli meats that she invariably brought for lunch), and an appreciation of the Go-Go's hits from the 1980's.

In the beginning of her school year with us, Lucy could do no wrong in my eyes. If she chose to do a tap dance on my head before unpacking her bag and putting her friends in the closet for the day (friends meaning transitional objects, dolls the size of small ponies), it was fine by me as long as she apologized for doing so. She always apologized. Her endearing manner, along with my love for the child and my four months total experience working with this population of students, made it difficult for me to pinpoint the functions of her behaviors. Consequently, it was impossible for me to consistently follow through on behavior plans implemented for "special" times like these.

It wasn't until one rainy day when the playground was off limits due to the weather that I became more aware of the driving forces behind some of her behaviors. As I pried her little fingers and toes off of the chain-link fence, the roundhouse punches I received in the back somehow helped to clearly spell out the function of the tantrums to me. From that day on, I referred to Lucy as "Spidergirl" in my head. Who knew that a 40-pound girl could be that agile up a ten foot fence? Nonetheless, this event marked the beginning of my awakening to the wondrous world of noncompliant behavior. With my eyes open and my being more cognizant of Lucy's behavior during activities she considered unpalatable, I was able to generalize my knowledge from the fence to the classroom. Things I heard in training suddenly made sense in a way that they never had before.

As I became more adept and confident of my abilities during discrete trial teaching, my interest in it grew. I understood how and when to reinforce, redirect, and ignore behavior during these times. The outstanding team I worked with must have really liked me that year: it was more often than not that I was designated Lucy's therapist for the morning. For the most part, Lucy worked for primary reinforcers. She seemed to have a natural inclination for Nerds ™. Sharing a love of Nerds ™ helped afford Lucy and me a pretty good working relationship. For every five pennies she earned, she got to enjoy a few candies from the bag her mother supplied. My cut was an overflowing handful from the bag my mom supplied for me. Sue me, I was jealous. These lovely candies were a welcome change from the M & M's™ that been the main staple of my daytime diet for the four previous months.

Even with my newfound knowledge of appropriate reinforcement, I sometimes let Lucy's funny disposition cloud my better judgement. In one particular instance, Lucy was experiencing some difficulty learning the correct verbal labels for foods. Her initial response, "rat dogs" upon being presented with a picture of frankfurters, was both funny and inventive to me. My natural response was to laugh. At this time, however, I failed to realize that my laughter was reinforcing to Lucy, thus increasing the chances that she would give me "rat dogs" as a response in the future. I tried to redeem myself a few weeks later in the cafeteria when I spotted another child eating a hot dog for lunch. I marched Lucy right up to that hot dog and took advantage of the situation to incidentally teach her the label. The only drawback to this reinforcing learning experience was my hastiness: I jumped at the chance to quickly work with a real hot dog (rather than a picture), never explaining to the other child what we were doing. The instance was a prime example of how a "making every minute count" teacher mentality, combined with the drive to be a good behavior therapist, can make you look even more bizarre than you really are.

At the onset of our working relationship, Lucy's mood and attitude towards programming seemed to be somewhat inconsistent and dependent upon other classroom stimuli. Redirecting her attention was a challenge when my opponents were a computer and a perpetual humming perseveration coming from a student on the other side of the room. A typical program run during these "distracting" times consisted of massed trials: my presentation of a stimulus, Lucy's echolalia of that stimulus, and my prompt of the correct response - over and over again. Initially, I found this process tiring and flustering. One day, Lucy would recite her entire family tree, and the next day to be her younger sister when asked "Who are *you*?" (with full verbal modeling for the correct response) during a social questions program.

Michelle, the brilliant and supportive teacher I was working under at that time, would usually sense my psychological stress. She would then award me *my* five pennies (although I know I could've held out for ten) for a "break" to run programs with other students, picking up where I had left off with Lucy. She was my savior; she allowed me to regain a sound mind in a sound body for the time being. What I didn't know then was that my leaving the situation was an opportunity for Lucy to perceive *me* the way I sometimes saw her - as inconsistent.

In the months to come, she would win some noncompliance power struggles, but lose some as well. The unfortunate circumstance was that she knew this. Her behavior eventually carried over into the large group instruction setting as well, where I had to beg, borrow, and steal just to get her to write her name on an assignment, secretly wishing to be a primary reinforcer just to see some results. Michelle, in contrast, would enter the scene, point to where Lucy's name should be written, and there it was. Lucy worked differently for Michelle because she was *consistent*. She had the ability and self-control to laugh and have fun with Lucy, as well as to redirect and ignore attention-seeking behaviors at the *appropriate times* to do so.

With this clear in my mind, I realized it was time to alter the type of relationship Lucy and I had, and from that moment on, I tried to follow in Michelle's footsteps as best I could. She was just that good at what she did. I made a promise to myself to develop the nurturing yet firm relationship she had with her students with my own future class. From that day forth, I saw myself as a relentless presenter of S^Ds, a master fader of prompts, letting no echolalia or noncompliance get in the way of a reciprocal conversation. I started using the errorless learning strategy religiously, and my favorite article of clothing became a

"Try Again" t-shirt. Now, a year and a half later, I've worked up the persistence and stamina to endure the sound of my own voice in order to successfully work through programs with students displaying task-avoidant behaviors. The distinct difference between then and now are the *results* I get from being consistent.

The point I've been driving at here, the importance of consistency, is related to some unforgettable advice I once received from the Dark Overlord of Applied Behavior Analysis: <u>Pick the battles you can win</u>. Never get into a behavior treatment plan where you can't follow through on your prompts or the consequences outlined by the treatment plan. The student will just learn to ignore your verbal prompts, and continue with the inappropriate behavior. Systematically increase the scope of your efforts as you gain control over the variables controlling behavior. As you do this, your consistency will lead to growth for all involved.

This chapter is inspired by those who helped me learn all there is to know, with special thanks to Mom, Bobby, Dana, and Laura.

Chapter Twelve: Teaching Samuel that
Talking Isn't That Bad
Kari Ann Dunlop

Samuel began at our ABA preschool for children with autistic spectrum disorders as an Early Intervention student in August, at the age of 26 months. When he entered our program, we could identify approximately five words that Samuel was using functionally (given a high motivation level). Generally, Samuel used these words in an echolalic fashion, usually repeating after an adult. When it was clear that he wanted juice, for example, his parents would say, "Say juice," and then Samuel might repeat "juice."

At that time, to communicate his needs, Samuel would usually take your hand and lead you to whatever he wanted, or he would bring the object to you. If he wanted juice, he might bring an empty cup and put it in your hand, or he would take your hand and lead you to the refrigerator. His parents remembered that when he was about thirteen months of age, Samuel had approximately thirty spontaneous words, which he used clearly and frequently for labeling.

On his first day in program, Samuel began discrete trial training with a few key goals. These included eye contact, imitating actions, and imitating words. At the time, we were probing to see what type of language Samuel would use with us. It took five days for him to imitate any words in discrete trials, and that day he said "book" three times. He didn't say it again for many weeks, however. After trying to have him imitate "book" for almost a month, we decided to try a more reinforcing word and asked him to say "cracker." If he said "cracker," Samuel was allowed to eat one. On the first day running "cracker" in trials, Samuel said "cracker" once, and then for four days all he did was look at us when we asked him to say the word. Obviously the cracker wasn't as desirable as we thought it would be!

We were not discouraged, however. This child would learn to talk when asked to. We switched to imitating "popcorn" after trying cracker with little success for one week. Again, Samuel had no intention of talking when we asked him to and he didn't say "popcorn" for three days. Then, suddenly on the fourth day, he very clearly said, "corn." This did not happen just once - Samuel imitated us three times that day (we were more than happy to accept "corn" as an adequate approximation of "popcorn"). Once Samuel imitated the word "popcorn" in order to get popcorn, we eliminated popcorn from his diet so it would be a very desirable treat that he would receive only after requesting it. Samuel had shown us that he could definitely say "popcorn," so we now required this verbalization in order for him to obtain the potent reinforcer. After nine days of imitating "popcorn," and consistently receiving the desired reinforcement (popcorn, of course) Samuel met criteria!

The day before we changed cracker to popcorn, we also added "Mamma" into his verbal imitation program. We knew from his parents that Samuel was fairly likely to say "Mamma," especially after it had been modeled. If he said "Mamma," he was given a picture of his family that he seemed to enjoy immensely. On the first day, he said "Mamma" six times, which seemed great to us. Samuel's motivation dropped off for a few days, but he still imitated "Mamma" an average of three or four times a day. After just over two weeks (and after the breakthrough with popcorn) Samuel began to consistently imitate "Mamma" in trials.

"Popcorn" and "Mamma" were the only two words Samuel successfully imitated in discrete trial training. As soon as Samuel consistently imitated these words, we moved the words to the *labeling objects goal* where we asked him, "What's this?" instead of prompting, "Say Mamma." The addition of words to his labeling objects goal went very quickly. The list follows:

popcorn (9/28/99)

Mamma (9/29/99)

Daddy (10/5/99)

bubbles (10/6/99)

cracker and candy (10/12)

car (10/13)

ball (10/14)

book (10/15)

puppy, milk, raisin, crayon, blanket (10/18)

plate, plane, boat, chair, spoon, shoe (10/21)

bear, bag, horse, cup, cow, pig, cookie (10/27)

shirt, pants, pretzel (11/1)

boots, coat (11/10)

knife, fork, pan, bed (11/16)

bread, comb, duck, chicken, wagon, block, apple (11/17/99)

The goal moved from discrete trials to maintenance on November 19th, after he had shown mastery of labeling 40 objects in trials. Maintenance involved running the goal only once a week to see if Samuel was able to retain his labeling capabilities with less practice. Labeling objects then moved to generalization on December 6th. During generalization, Samuel was taken around the school and asked to label any object that a teacher showed him. These objects included some of the 40 that he originally learned in discrete trial training, but he was also expected to be able to label other common objects. Samuel successfully completed the goal of labeling objects on December 15th, almost four months after he enrolled in our program, and less than three months since he started the goal.

Once the consistency of discrete trial training became familiar and understandable to Samuel, he progressed very quickly in his language. His ability to generalize became immediately apparent. Words were added almost daily and he became able to imitate words across any setting. He was again spontaneously labeling objects that he saw around him, just as he had done when he was about thirteen months of age.

When he started with us, Samuel had no desire to talk. We believed that he could talk, however. It was through steady discrete trial training and immediate reinforcement that Samuel realized that speaking was easier and more rewarding than not speaking. Once we were able to break through his noncompliant behavior and encourage him to talk, he moved along quickly. Initially, Samuel needed a great deal of immediate and potent reinforcement to encourage his spontaneous language. Now, however, he seems to truly enjoy talking and expressing himself throughout his day.

Chapter Thirteen: Rachel Loses Six Months:
Considering Medication Use
Bobby Newman

It was a Monday in April of 1988 when Rachel said to me, "Remember what I did this weekend?" I must have gone a little pale. I hadn't worked with Rachel over a weekend since autumn. By April, I saw her only on weekdays at a residence where I was doing some counseling. I had a hunch what she was getting at though, so I played along. "What did you do, Rachel?"

"I threw the soda on your jacket!"

Damn. I was right. She was back on Haldol and her mom hadn't told us.

What Rachel was displaying was a phenomenon known as "state dependency." She had been taking the psychotropic medication Haldol when she had thrown the soda on my jacket. That was several months ago. She had gone off the Haldol shortly after that, and apparently now was taking it again. Her memories of the intervening period had, in a real sense, been wiped clean. It was as if she had lost several months of her life from her memory (the period in between Haldol-usage periods).

Such extreme reactions to medications are not commonplace. One does see a variety of unintended effects of medications, however, from "Ritalin rebounds" to drug-induced hazes where the child seems too weak to stand, right through berserk rages where the student seems to lose all impulse control. Particularly frustrating is the medication variable when it comes to behavioral programming. I need the same person with me every day if I'm to create consistent behavior treatment plans. If he is a different kid each week because his medications are different, or are being given at a different level, or are "wearing off" and "wearing on" during the course of the day, programming becomes nearly impossible. A different brain chemistry often means that your programming has largely been lost. A child may be really focused at ten in the morning, and completely unreachable by noon due to the waxing and waning of medications.

It is also not uncommon to see children (or adults) on laundry lists of medications: "He's on this so he won't be too aggressive. It makes him a little sluggish, though, so he's on this so he won't get too drowsy. This one is for his obsessions, and this one is to control the side effects of that one and. . ." Who is the child, and what is the behavior? What is the effect of the medications and what is the result of his disability? I get lost in there somewhere. It's sometimes enough to make you want to throw the whole collection of medicines into the ocean and hope they don't poison the marine life. Sometimes I feel like shouting, "You've got two choices. He can be awake or he can be asleep. Take your pick, but thinking that this medication is going to just eliminate the aggressive behavior without a plan and without side-effects is a fantasy!"

So, is there any use for psychotropic medication when dealing with the autistic-spectrum disorders? That depends on who you talk to. Some people really recommend them, while other programs don't allow them at all. Let's talk about how to make responsible decisions.

First off, let's realize that there is no drug specifically designed and proven effective for autism. Every few months, someone publishes a study or goes on television to claim positive effects from some medication or other. Realize, however, that these are not medications that were specifically designed for autism. Often, it is a supposedly serendipitous use of a medication designed for another disorder. Also, such claims are sometimes the result of the "symptomatic" use of medications (e.g., "He has obsessions and compulsions, so I'll give him a drug for obsessive-compulsive disorder.").

Whoops, hold on! Notice the sleight of hand I just performed. Yes, he has obsessions and compulsions. They are the result of his autistic-spectrum diagnosis, however, and not the result of "true" OCD. To take another example, it is sometimes said that depressed people become anorexic. That just means they stop eating. That's very different from saying that they develop *anorexia nervosa*, which is the name of the eating disorder characterized by disturbed body image and fear of gaining weight. Just because the same word is used doesn't mean that the same cause is there or that the same medication will be useful. As you Led Zeppelin fans know, sometimes words have two meanings. Autism and attention-deficit disorder share difficulties in focusing as a characteristic. For this reason, medications usually associated with attention-deficit disorder (e.g., Ritalin) are often tried with people with autistic-spectrum disorders. Sometimes it can help, but much more frequently it does not. Just remember that we're shooting in the dark, and you know what often happens when you do that.

We must be careful, though. There is such a thing as dual diagnosis. It is entirely possible that the individual will have another psychiatric disturbance superimposed on top of the autistic-spectrum diagnosis. Being autistic does not give you an immunity from other disorders (e.g., depression). If there is truly another disorder at work, and if there is an empirically validated medication for that disorder, you may do well to try it. Keep in mind, though, that you are giving a medication aimed at the second diagnosis, and not particularly at the autistic-spectrum disorder.

It is also true that sometimes people with autism respond to other medications, even if there isn't a second diagnosis. It can happen. Once, about three years ago, I saw a child whose performance on her discrete trial programs took off once they tried her on Prozac. I was quite amazed, as I hadn't known she was on the anti-depressant, and saw a huge jump in performance I couldn't explain. After discussing the little girl's sudden increase in performance with her mom, she confided in the staff that she was trying Prozac with her daughter. I was, of course, pleased that the drug was working, although I wished she had told us. What if the child had to go to the hospital and we didn't know she was on Prozac and the doctors gave her something that interacted badly with it?

To be honest, for every one such child who makes improvements, I have seen literally hundreds of parents who try medications for their children with no effect, or even disastrous results (behaviorally speaking). How do you know if your child will be the one who will benefit? You can't. Therefore, we have to proceed very carefully, as scientists.

Let's assume that you want to try a medication, or your doctor suggests one. How can you assess its effects? Happily, a good ABA program gives you all you need to proceed. There will be a great deal of behavioral data that preceded the medication. You can use that as your baseline levels of inappropriate behavior and rates of skill acquisition on programs. Try the medication for a period of time and use the data from teaching programs and behavior treatment plans as your measures of effectiveness. Too often, people use very subjective measures. "He seems better, more focused" is the phrase I usually hear. Look at the data, however, and we see that the assessment is a hopeful placebo effect, and not a real effect. Make sure you are collecting very careful observations. It is sometimes not enough just to track your target behavior. Yes, "stims" and aggression may be way down. That may be, however, because the child is so medicated that he can barely move. I could achieve the same effect with a good sledge hammer. That's not exactly a desirable treatment modality.

We may also have to look at the potential side-effects of the medications as well. A student may begin to tic, twirl his hair, become incontinent, or engage in other behaviors once he starts the medication; behaviors that he never displayed before. Observations will also have to be systematically collected throughout the day. As mentioned above, the student may be very different after lunch, when his medication levels may be wearing off. Time-released medication or multiple, smaller, dosages throughout the day may have to be considered. Remember, we aren't talking about aspirin. The medication may not show its full effects for several weeks. You must be systematic and avoid the temptation to "give him an extra one" when it seems he might have a bad day. These are not drugs to play with, they can have serious effects on the nervous system.

If I can give any solid advice, it would be to try behavior treatment plans first. If nothing works after a solid period of several months of trying plans and carrying them out properly, then you might consider medication usage. Just remember to proceed with caution and in an empirically valid way. Just like the behavior treatment plans, medication trials are an experiment. Be sure to also make sure you know what you are giving and WHY you are giving it. Medications are not aimed at "making him better." They are meant to address specific issues. Medications may be aimed at decreasing perseveration or obsessions or excessive agitation. They are not aimed at "making him better."

I apologize that I can't make this a happy story with Rachel, the way most of the stories in this book series have been. By the time I left the residence where Rachel was living, she was more "out of it" than ever. She had been on more medications than I could count, many simultaneously. She paced for hours at a time and engaged in aggression and endless mumbling. She resisted attempts at interaction and laughed and cried for no apparent reason. At times she saw things and heard things that weren't there. She lost skills she had learned over the years and didn't learn new ones. I left work many days feeling like I was going to throw up.

I remember one particularly miserable night. Rachel had attacked her sister during a visit, and had attacked her roommate as the woman slept. She had cut her roommate so badly that the woman needed stitches in her head. The next day, I went to the residence and drove with staff to a psychiatric hospital where we hoped they would "dry her out" and reassess medication so that we could begin treatment plans on solid ground. When we went to the hospital, Rachel looked over at me and said, "But I was good today! I didn't do anything bad!" I knew she needed medical attention, and I wasn't going to wait for the next attack, which might well have sent someone else to the emergency room. Nonetheless, I felt sick as I explained to Rachel that they were going to help her to get a better medication regime.

Let's call my nausea a side-effect of the medications she was on.

Chapter Fourteen: Mikie Puts his Coat Away
Dina Douglass

We characterize behavior as prompt-dependent when a behavior is within a child's repertoire, but is not displayed by the student unless someone delivers a prompt for the response (e.g., a student who does not begin eating when food is presented, until and unless he is specifically told to begin). It is quite possibly the most frustrating and tedious behavioral characteristic one finds oneself dealing with when teaching some students diagnosed with autistic-spectrum disorders.

Mikie, one of the students at the preschool for children with autistic-spectrum disorders where I was employed at the time of this treatment   plan, would be characterized as extremely prompt-dependent. Mikie was four years old and had recently transferred from another preschool, one which did not utilize ABA methodology. According to initial observations, Mikie appeared to be fairly low functioning. The operative word here, though, is definitely "appeared." It said in his records that he was non-verbal and did not possess many skills. Don't believe everything you read.

One day shortly after he joined our program, while walking down the hall to the bathroom, Mikie began to spontaneously label pictures on the wall - "Big Bird," "flower," "tree," etc. We were astonished and began to look at his behavior even more closely. We began to notice that when he thought no one was looking, he was actually quite verbal (e.g., singing or echolating videos when he thought no one was within hearing range).

I began to adjust Mikie's programs within the discrete trial setting (e.g., adding a labeling program that he actually came to enjoy). I began to notice, however, that Mikie looked for prompting when we were doing drills. This posed a difficult problem. When the request to clap hands was given, for example, Mikie would reach for our hands and cover his in ours in order for us to clap for him. He would clap only as far as our hands would allow it. If we dropped our hands before he finished clapping, he too would drop his hands. It was clear that physical prompting no longer could be used due to Mikie becoming dependent on it to perform his skills. From that point on, only the very least intrusive prompt could be used. This meant that instead of fully taking his hands in ours, we would either tap his elbows or pull at his sleeves. We had to work on fading prompts in as accelerated a fashion as possible. We faded to gestural prompts whenever a prompt was needed, avoiding the physical contact. We changed to a "waiting game" for verbal programs. The prompt, "what's this?" was delivered and Mikie was required to label an item. If he did not respond after one verbal prompt, we would hold the item and wait for him to respond. After several sessions, Mikie began to label. We made sure to use reinforcing items as stimuli in these early stages to heighten motivation.

In addition to using reinforcing stimuli, it is important to note that we had very potent reinforcing consequences once he did respond. These reinforcers served to keep up motivation, and worked their way into our fading procedure. Rather than giving Mikie verbal prompts to perform a skill, we simply reminded him that he was "working for <u>fill in the blank</u>." Also during this time, we found that Mikie satiated on reinforcers very quickly. After receiving a reinforcer two or three times, he grew tired of it. It was therefore very important to keep a variety of reinforcers handy. We also gave him the opportunity to choose what reinforcers he wanted to work for before starting the program. These procedures were implemented throughout Mikie's entire day, including hanging his coat in his cubby (bringing us to our case study).

Upon arrival, Mikie would walk around the classroom rather than going over to his cubby. Once he was redirected to his cubby, he would take off his coat and place it on the floor. When verbally prompted to pick up his coat, he would hand it to a staff member, place it on the floor, or hold it in his hand with his arm extended toward his cubby. I decided we should extinguish Mikie's prompt dependency here as well as in his discrete trial work. One verbal directive would be given to him to place his coat in his cubby. If he did not respond, he would be physically directed to his cubby and we would wait for him to hang up his coat independently.

The first day, I was prepared for a long wait. I placed Mikie in front of his cubby, gave him the directive to hang up his coat and waited. . . and waited. . . and waited. I pulled up a chair, turned my back to him, and wrote up lesson plans covering the next few weeks. Mikie stood near his cubby, although at times he attempted to leave the area. If this occurred, I simply placed him back in front of his cubby. Two and one half hours later, Mikie hung up his coat. All of the staff were elated, and we all cheered and delivered reinforcement by taking turns swinging him in the air. The next two days went pretty much the same way, which gave me a much-needed opportunity to catch up on some paperwork.

The fourth day, however, went differently. Mikie threw a wrench into my nicely laid-out and prepared plan. I placed him in front of his cubby as I had previously, which was actually easier than it had been. The problem was that instead of just standing there, or even attempting to leave and go to the toy area, he began to find standing by the cubby reinforcing. He began to perseverate by visually tracking the lines of the cubby while running his finger across it and singing. I remembered that even the best laid plans, with the best intentions, could fail. It was obvious that I needed to rethink this strategy, and fast. Still keeping in mind Mikie's tendency towards the development of prompt-dependency and not wanting to physically prompt his behavior, my next move was to use an overcorrection procedure. When one uses overcorrection, the student is prompted to correct the environmental effects of his/her misbehavior and/or to practice appropriate forms of behavior (Foxx, 1982).

I sat next to Mikie, and gave him the verbal directive to hang up his coat. Once he did not respond, I took his coat, placed it in myself and said, "This is putting your coat in the cubby." I then handed the coat back to him. This was repeated several hundred times, until after two hours and fifteen minutes, he did it independently (actually a great relief to me). In retrospect, as his average time of placing his coat in his cubby prior to this was about two hours, we actually hadn't lost any time. We carried out the procedure every day over the next week, and noted that the latency to Mikie putting his coat away decreased each day. Finally, one day he walked in and hung up his coat after only *one* verbal directive.

As I was such a glutton for punishment, I decided that I would work on each article of clothing, including his lunch box. I felt this was an important task, as it was part of a classroom routine and he needed to learn how to follow routines. Thankfully, his skills generalized and we had no such issues with the other items. He put them away quite independently.

(Not from Bobby Newman: this is a more common problem than

people realize, as we tend to over-prompt in general. We don't even realize that we're over-prompting and, in so doing, taking away the chance for the student to learn to perform skills independently. A great teacher I had the pleasure to work with was Gretchen van Dijk. We worked through a similar case of a student who would stand in front of his cubby and repeat "hang up your coat" until someone said "yes." Once we realized we were feeding into his prompt-dependency, we were mute when he used his phrase. The inevitable extinction burst occurred and I lost track of how many times he said it during treatment. On quiet nights, I think I can still hear it. I'll bet Gretch can, too.)

Chapter Fifteen: Who's Afraid of the Big Bad Wolf. . .and the Dentist, and the Hairdresser, and the Birthday Cake, and the. . .

Randy Horowitz

Children with autism often engage in problem behavior when asked to participate in activities to which they are infrequently exposed. In many cases, the problem behavior serves as a means to avoid an unpleasant situation or to communicate a need. This, combined with fears associated with dentists, doctors, hairdressers and their corresponding scary paraphernalia, prevents some children with autism from learning appropriate skills and behaviors related to these activities.

Because of these problem behaviors, parents and teachers tend to avoid these situations. Or, minimally, they create accommodations and modifications that disguise the situations. They disguise to the point that replication of the same set of circumstances for subsequent teaching opportunities are generally impossible. These "in the meantime strategies" may be helpful, for a short while, but will get more and more difficult as children get older and bigger.

The following short tales describe interventions that were successful in teaching a number of young children with autism to tolerate birthday parties, haircuts, dental exams, and so on. These tales are laced with commonalities. In all cases, functional assessment revealed that the children demonstrated problem behavior in order to escape aversive and fear-provoking situations. The following key ingredients were implemented to systematically teach appropriate skills and behavior and, in so doing, to reduce fear:

1.   task analysis
2.   practice, practice, practice
3.   systematic desensitization
4.   practice, practice, practice
5.   reinforcement
6.   practice, practice, practice
7.   differential reinforcement
8.   practice, practice, practice
9.   shaping
10.   practice, practice, practice

Finally, skills related to tolerating birthday parties, dental exams and haircuts were practiced in analog settings (school and home) prior to generalization to the real place.

It's NOT My Birthday and I'll Cry If I Want To

There's a boy at a birthday party

And he's hiding under the table

"Oh No," yelled the teachers

"Yes, yes," screamed the boy

Dwindle, dwindle went the candle flames

"No way," cried the boy as he ran out of the classroom

This was a scene from a birthday party that took place in a preschool class for students with autism. No, this boy was not afraid of flames. In fact, the only negative history he had with candles was that each time somebody ELSE blew them out, he got very upset. More than upset; he engaged in tantrums that lasted far longer than most birthday parties.

Well, with only 6 kids in the class and 3 staff, birthday parties were not a daily event, not even monthly. You may be thinking that that was a good thing. At times, the teachers thought so, too. Although waiting for the next birthday party and crossing their fingers and praying for better behavior were proactive thoughts, the teachers knew it was not going to provide little Jake with enough opportunities to practice appropriate behavior.

So, in the name of fair play, the teachers (with parental consent) decided to create as many opportunities for Jake to practice tolerating others blowing out candles as they provided him opportunities to learn other skills. After all, Jake required at least 10 trials a day to learn to label a color and to identify a number. Skills like answering and asking questions required even more opportunities to practice.

Suffice it to say that this classroom became a birthday party haven. Lots of singing, lots of cake, lots of presents and, most importantly, lots of chances for Jake to learn to tolerate others blowing out the candles. Creating these opportunities for practice was just one ingredient. The first plan was that a teacher would sit next to Jake at the party and be ready, willing and able to quickly give Jake a lick of the cake frosting the SECOND his peer blew out the candles if, and only if, he was seated at the table quietly. This turned out to not be quick enough, as Jake began his tantrum after the verse, ". . . happy birthday to you" and a split second before a peer blew out the candles.

Plan B was the first step to ultimate success. This plan involved a teacher and Jake playing the 1:1 blowing out the candle game. Jake and the teacher sang the song. Jake was told that if he let the teacher blow out one candle first, he would be permitted to blow out the rest AS LONG AS HE WAS SEATED AT THE TABLE QUIETLY!!! It took several teaching opportunities until Jake was blowing out systematically fewer candles than the teacher, and until finally, it was the teacher's turn only. Once Jake tolerated this 1:1 game, then back to the birthday party arena he went. With a dense schedule of reinforcement for sitting quietly while someone ELSE blew out the candles and many, many opportunities to practice, Jake learned to tolerate birthday parties. During a follow up mock birthday party some months later, Jake was even observed encouraging his peers to blow out the candles.

"Say Ah": Not Just for Verbal Imitation Anymore

There's a boy at the dentist office

And he's hiding under the chair

"Oh No," yelled the dentist

"Yes, yes," screamed the boy

Buzz, buzz went the drill

"No way," cried the boy as he ran out of the room

Not only couldn't Sam tolerate the big, bad scary dentist, toothbrushing often looked like a wrestling match (you know the default headlock maneuver one resorts to when all else fails). Remember the birthday party tale and the point about limited opportunities to practice? Well, the same holds true for visits to the dentist. Once every 6-9 months is NOT nearly enough time for some children with autism to learn a skill and related appropriate behavior.

Sam's teachers began by systematically desensitizing Sam to toothbrushing. Minimally, this skill gets practiced twice a day. Still not enough! So, upon arrival into class, after snack, after lunch and prior to dismissal, Sam was provided with opportunities to learn to tolerate toothpaste, toothbrushing, and ultimately all of the dental utensils. The only thing Sam's parents were asked not to do was practice the headlock maneuver at any time while this teaching program was being run in school. The reason? We wanted to avoid any aversive stimuli associated with dental hygiene. In other words, break the chain of resisting and protesting. Teaching a whole new repertoire of appropriate skills and behavior in school first, then generalizing to home and then to THE DENTIST OFFICE was the plan.

Sam's teachers and parents created a detailed task analysis of all the steps included in a toothbrushing routine. Sam practiced each step in a traditional discrete trial format until it was mastered. Once criterion was met, the next step was introduced and so on and so on. When Sam completed toothbrushing with 100% accuracy in school, mom was invited to come to school and practice this skill with Sam. He had no problem generalizing these skills and behaviors with mom, so he was then permitted to practice the skill at home with mom and dad. No problem!! The same procedures were then implemented to teach Sam to tolerate a dental exam.

Here is the program that Sam's mom and teachers developed to desensitize Sam to the dentist. Please keep in mind that each child is unique and this program may have to be altered to meet the needs of your child. The key to the success of this program was, once again, creating enough opportunities for this skill to be practiced. In addition, mastery of the necessary skills in an analog setting (the classroom) was required before participation in the actual dentist office.

Program: Dentist Visit and Exam

It may be helpful to forward this program to the dentist prior to the intervention. As you may need to practice a particular step with great frequency, set up several appointments a couple of days apart. Visiting the dentist at a time when the office is less crowded, like the last appointment of the day, is favorable.

Target behavior: When presented with the instruction, "Time to go see the dentist," the child will go with mom to the exam room, sit quietly, follow dentist directions and tolerate all steps of the dental exam (in the absence of refusal to open mouth and other "non-compliant" and disruptive behavior)

Some prerequisite skills:
1.   sits in chair
2.   imitates adult movements
3.   follows simple directions
4.   tolerates toothbrushing

Criteria: Non-compliant and disruptive behavior must be at zero levels on a target step in order to move to the subsequent steps at the next visit.

Program procedure:
1.   Mom gives S^D, "Time to see the dentist"
2.   Child walks into the exam room (Note: In some cases a program must be designed to teach the child to tolerate entering the dentist office and waiting in the waiting room. These were

not problem steps for Sam).

3. Sits in the dentist chair

4. Wears a smock (Note Again: In some cases a program must be designed to teach the child to tolerate wearing the smock. Practice this at home or school first!)

5. Tolerates the light being shined in his mouth

6. Opens mouth for mirror

7. Allows dentist to look in mouth

8. Opens mouth for pick

9. Allows pick to touch each tooth

10. Opens mouth for toothbrush

11. Allows dentist to brush all teeth

12. Opens mouth for tooth cleaner

13. Allows dentist to perform full cleaning

14. Opens mouth for scraper

15. Allows scraper to touch all teeth

Reinforcement: Appropriate sitting and following directions should be reinforced with verbal praise and tokens on a continuous schedule throughout the exam. At the end of the exam (the number of steps practiced varies), the child should receive a tangible reward.

Criteria for mastery of the entire program: The child must exhibit "cooperative behavior" for all steps of the dental exam for 2 consecutive appointments.

To ensure generalization and maintenance, have the child

sit in a different chair each time and, upon mastery of the entire program, schedule dentist visits every 2-3 weeks, then every 4-5 weeks etc.

A Bad Hair Day: More like a bad hair year. . . or two

There's a boy in the hair salon

And he's hiding under the counter

"Oh No," yelled the beautician

"Yes, yes," screamed the boy

Snip, snip went the scissors

"No way," cried the boy as he ran out of the salon

Jake always had the coolest, trendiest hairstyles. This was no small feat, considering his level of difficulty tolerating a haircut. Prior to implementation of the systematic procedures outlined in this tale, numerous strategies were employed to get Jake to engage in appropriate behavior during a haircut. These strategies ranged from dad cutting his hair while he was sleeping to distracting Jake by having him watch a favorite movie while getting a haircut. And, of course, the default headlock maneuver was consistently implemented in efforts to achieve a successful outcome.

Jake's parents and teachers recognized that the above outlined strategies were good "in the meantime" options. But, in the long run, was Jake learning the appropriate skills necessary to successfully participate in haircuts? Jake's parents and teachers knew the answer was "no." This meant that Jake would need to overcome his fear by learning to tolerate each step of a haircut. This needed to be accomplished first by teaching Jake to tolerate his hair being brushed and combed. (Just like little Sam needed to tolerate toothbrushing prior to dental exams.) His teachers, to determine what particular steps of the haircut were aversive, conducted careful assessments in Jake's class. Results of the assessment revealed that he did not like a variety of things associated with a haircut. Included on the "bad list" were; tilting his head backward to have his hair washed, wearing a smock and having snips of hair fall from the scissors and on to his face.

Upon mastery of a program called "Tolerating Hairbrush," Jake's teacher's and mom implemented the "Tolerating Haircut" program (detailed below for your adaptation and use). It is important to keep in mind that mock haircuts occurred in school as part of Jake's daily programming. During the time it took Jake to master each step in school, mom was discouraged from bringing Jake to the hair salon. Again, we wanted to break the chain of problem behavior associated with haircuts that began the moment mom turned left onto the street where the salon was located. The desire to begin with a clean slate and establish a whole new set of circumstances far exceeded the commitment to a particular hair stylist.

As with the dental exam, many appointments were

scheduled in advance. Although some steps needed to be repeated over subsequent visits, the end result of this long road yielded a kid who continued to have the coolest, trendiest haircuts, without the hassles.

Program: Tolerating a Haircut

Target Behavior: When presented with the instruction, "Time for a haircut", the child will go with mom to the barbershop and sit quietly (with no instances of aggression and disruptive behavior) while the hairdresser cuts his hair.

Some prerequisite skills:

1.   sits in a chair

2.   imitates adult movements

3.   follows simple one concept commands

4.   cooperation with haircut in analog setting (classroom)

Criteria: Aggressive and disruptive behavior must be at zero levels on a target step in order to move to subsequent steps at he next visit.

Program procedure:

1.   Mom gives instruction, "Time for a haircut"

2.   Child walks into salon, walks over to chair where haircut will eventually take place, and greets the hairdresser.

3.   Above and sit in chair for 2 minutes (may need to set timer)

4.   Above and sit in chair for 5 minutes

5.   Above and tolerates wearing smock for 5 minutes

6.   Smock on, wet hair (with spray bottle) and hairdresser combs hair

7.   Above plus 2 snips in front and 2 snips on back

8.   Above plus complete haircut

Reinforcement:

Appropriate sitting and direction following should be reinforced with verbal praise and tokens on a continuous schedule throughout the haircut. The child may be taken for a treat only if he/she demonstrates "cooperative behavior" during each step of the program.

*Note: some children may require more frequent and immediate reinforcement.

Criteria for mastery of the entire program: Child must exhibit "cooperative behavior" for all steps of the haircut for 3 consecutive weeks. (All steps are to be performed successfully 3 times in a row on separate occasions)

     To ensure generalization and maintenance: Have child sit in a different chair each time. You may want to probe with a different hairdresser in the same salon. Schedule haircuts every 2-3 weeks, then every 3-4 weeks and so on. (It may not be necessary to do all steps of the program, just trim bangs etc.)

     In summary, I would like to stress the importance of teaching children with autism the skills and behaviors associated with the above mentioned real life activities. Data based decisions about including children with autism into less structured school settings are carefully made by parents and professionals. It is equally important to systematically design programs that will set the foundation for successful inclusive opportunities outside of the classroom. Regardless of where children spend their school career, and whether or not they participate in academic activities with their typical peers, one thing is for certain; all children with autism need dental exams and haircuts and most will be invited to birthday parties. So, it is the responsibility of parents and professionals to include these skill acquisition programs in their children's individualized curriculum.

In addition to dental exams, birthday parties and haircuts, children with autism are required to participate in other activities outside of the home and classroom. The procedures outlined in this chapter may also be employed to teach children with autism to successfully participate in a variety of real life activities. Through systematic teaching and gradual exposure, children with autism can learn a myriad of skills including: increasing their repertoire of food, watching a movie in a dark scary theater and even visiting lions and tigers and bears at the zoo!

I realize that the rate of acquisition of these complex skills and behaviors varies across children. In some cases criteria for mastery may take weeks or even months. "In the meantime," remember to celebrate each successful step along the way!

Chapter Sixteen: What are Sisters Good for, Anyway?
Dana Reinecke

Marc is a beautiful little boy with a great smile. He loves to be tickled and thrown onto the couch, and really gets a big kick out of it when you blow your lips against his tummy. He's three years old, and he's autistic.

Marc had the good fortune to be born to parents who are intelligent, resourceful, and dedicated. Nothing is too much for them to do for this child. As the consultant in charge of his home program, I have to be careful to make my requests of his parents reasonable, because I know that they will stay up all night making materials, or writing to their Congress person, if I say "he needs it." It's a good thing that Marc's parents are so resourceful, because they have the unique blessings and stressors of being the parents of triplets.

Marc's sisters, Hannah and Grace, are as beautiful and engaging as he is. Each child is completely different from the other in personality and looks, and all together they are a wonderful family. In more ways than one, they are a home programmer's dream come true. Not only are the parents completely on-board with the program (Mom often corrects me when I don't remember my own programs), but there is an amazing opportunity for socialization with same-age, typically-developing peers built right into the house! I've been in many situations where I've had to make the awkward request that the parents get some friends with little kids so we can have some socialization opportunities. Here, all I have to do is ask, and I've got a built-in nursery school!

One of the first ways we took advantage of this situation was to set up a program for turn-taking. The concept was simple: Marc was required to sit quietly and wait for his turn at a variety of activities, such as jumping on a trampoline, putting pieces in a puzzle or pegs in a board, building with blocks, or rolling a ball. We deliberately varied the activities, so that we would be more likely to obtain generalization to real-life situations. Upon appropriately waiting for and taking his turn, he received reinforcers such as popcorn or fruit. Within a few weeks, instead of jumping around the room, pulling on his diaper, or babbling to himself, Marc was sitting quietly, actually watching his sisters! Today, he actually waits and takes turns better than Hannah or Grace. I guess I forgot to give reinforcers to some other people who needed them.

I didn't make that mistake with the next intervention the girls participated in. Because Marc was non-verbal, we had taught him to use the Picture Exchange Communication System (PECS). This involves handing over a picture of an object as a means of requesting. (Although it's really another story, I just have to put in here that Marc is the King of PECS, and eight months later, is starting to pair word approximations with the exchange.)

We incorporated PECS into a peer social situation by teaching Marc to give the picture to one of his sisters, who

116

would conveniently be holding a bowl of the reinforcer du jour. At first, Marc consistently handed the picture to the adult (me, his teachers, or his mom) who was facilitating the interaction. We consistently redirected him to hand the picture to Hannah or Grace, and eventually he began to spontaneously make requests of them. We taught Hannah and Grace to take the picture from him and to give him whatever it was he was asking for. In return for being such good helpers, they then got to take one for themselves. Truth be known, it became a "one for Marc, five for me," situation, but it worked. In fact, Marc began to use his PECS to make requests of his sisters *outside* of the teaching situation, when no adults were around! For the first time, he was seeking them out and making initiations to them.

Our next step was to teach Marc to imitate his sisters. We are currently working on translating this goal into parallel play. We started simply, with what we know works for Marc: face-to-face discrete-trial teaching. This time, however, the teachers were not highly-paid (not that they don't deserve it) early intervention providers, but three-year old girls. Hannah and Grace were taught to get Marc's eye contact, deliver the S^D (instruction) "Do this" and perform some action, and then deliver a reinforcer if he imitated their action. If he did not imitate the action, a teacher was right behind him to prompt the correct response. Again, the actions were varied to facilitate generalization, and Hannah and Grace's reward was a reinforcer every time they gave one to their brother.

In no time at all, Marc was attending closely to his sisters and imitating their actions in the discrete-trial setting. At the same time, Hannah and Grace became excellent ABA therapists. They initiated teaching opportunities with Marc on their own, outside of teaching hours. Today, either girl might turn to Marc while they are sitting on the couch, watching TV, and demand eye contact, prompt it if she doesn't get it, then deliver an S^D. Both girls are great about prompting when needed and delivering verbal praise. They have also generalized their skills to other programs, including verbal imitation and action commands. This was completely on their own; no one asked them to run extra trials in their spare time.

Well, Hannah and Grace definitely have careers in ABA if they want them in about 15 more years, but what has this done for Marc? Wonders. Where before he didn't even seem to know that his sisters existed, unless they were annoying him, he now looks at them, uses PECS to "talk" to them, and plays in close proximity to them. He follows them, crawls into their beds in the middle of the night, and shares toys with them. He forms a "train" with them, hands on the shoulders of the girl in front and allowing the one in back to put her hands on his shoulders. Marc is now a part of his family.

My theory of what happened here is that Marc's sisters acquired reinforcing value for him, by giving him other reinforcers. When a previously neutral stimulus, or something that doesn't have a strong value that is either positive or negative, is paired with a highly positive stimulus, that neutral stimulus can come to take on the value of the positive stimulus. To put it more simply, by associating something you really like with something you don't care much about, you are more likely to develop a fondness for the thing that you didn't care about.

This is a way of explaining why and how everyone comes to develop loving relationships. The newborn baby has few desires: milk, warmth, and dryness. Usually only one or two people take care of these needs at first. These people (Mom and Dad) become paired with milk, warmth, and dryness, and pretty soon Mom and Dad become desirable all on their own. Other people get associated with Mom and Dad, and they then become good, too. As the child gets more sophisticated, the important people in his or her life (who all go back to that first pairing of Mom and Dad with love, affection, and of course, milk) get paired with other neutral things, which become valuable. This could be how we develop our preferences for things we don't need to survive, like music, art, and leisure activities.

This process seems to be difficult for children with autism. They have a tougher time associating people with other reinforcers. Anyone who has worked with children diagnosed with this disorder has had the experience of seeing the previously aloof child become enamored of his therapists, while simultaneously ignoring or failing to notice his classmates. Maybe it's because the therapists are delivering high densities of reinforcement. The conclusion, to me, is simple: to get children with autism to like their peers, the peers should give reinforcers, too.

Marc's story is a powerful example of how well this can work, and how easily it can be integrated into a family's life. At this point, the density of primary reinforcement delivered by Hannah and Grace is dramatically reduced, but the good results keep happening. That must mean that Hannah and Grace are now reinforcers, too!

Chapter Seventeen: ABA = Robotic ?
Helen Bloomer

Throughout the past few years, the field of Applied Behavior Analysis has made extensive efforts to communicate to the public its accomplishments and successful results with regard to children with a diagnosis of autism. Yet, when I am consulting or providing a training to various consumers, at least one person always make the statement:

> "I've heard ABA turns children into robots and they only can talk in robotic fashion."

Of course, the component of ABA they are most likely referring to that supposedly creates robots is discrete trial training. And, of course, discrete trial training can indeed do this if the educational program only consists of this type of teaching. It is important to state in no uncertain terms then, that this is not an ABA program; it is a program that is merely implementing one component of ABA.

This type of incident occurred during a training I was invited to conduct for a group of preschool staff in upstate New York. Parents of a three-year old boy diagnosed with autism were very interested in creating an ABA program. Thus, the preschool he attended needed training.

The little boy, named Brent, participated each day in the

training during the "hands on" sessions. Brent exhibited limited cognitive and social skills, and did not yet have any verbal language. In addition, he engaged, with high frequency, in a variety of maladaptive behaviors. These included, but were not limited to, aggressive hitting, kicking, struggling and biting, self-injurious head-banging, biting and hair-pulling, active non-compliance and inappropriate vocalizations. As typically can happen during the initial stages of intervention, Brent rebelled. He did, however, begin to respond towards the end of the training week. So, after setting up a variety of instructional programs and coordinating data-collection procedures, the staff and parents began an intensive 40-hour per week ABA program. I continued to consult with the preschool, and monitor Brent's progress through e-mails, phone conferences, videotapes and site visits.

During the next couple of months, Brent made nice progress across all content areas except expressive language. Regardless of changes in reinforcement, play breaks, materials, staff or time of day that trials were run, Brent continued to engage in maladaptive behaviors with high frequency and intensity during these programs. So, during the next site consultation, I made the decision to increase the intensity of programming in the expressive language content area. I asked the parents and staff to begin implementing 3 sessions of 300 trials per day of verbal imitation. As you can imagine, they were aghast!

Within the week, however, Brent was imitating the first set of words with 70% appropriate responses. In addition, the presence of his maladaptive behaviors was significantly reduced! Within three months, Brent had a verbal vocabulary of 54 words. I continued to consult for Brent for the next two years. He made wonderful progress across all content areas, including expressive language.

At about this point, the parents were relocating to the Albany area. They decided to enroll him in the preschool program that I direct. For the first couple of days, Brent seemed quite bewildered by the change of environments; however, he quickly settled in. The staff could not help but comment how he came "to attention" whenever I walked into his classroom. One day in particular, he was quite concerned with my presence. He asked the teacher working with him, "Where's Helen?" She told him I had left to go to another classroom. Brent responded:

"Whew, now I can relax!"

Robotic? I think not.

Chapter Eighteen: Seeing the Forest for the Trees:
Musings on What Makes a Real Gain
Bobby Newman

One of the more distasteful duties I have found myself performing in recent years is that of "expert witness," appearing in court to give testimony about what ABA is and is not. It is generally a wasted exercise, as my fellow witnesses use and ignore literature to suit whatever end they are being paid to represent at that particular moment. A topic which inevitably comes up is that of "Lovaas." I can't begin to count how many times I've been asked to comment on the Lovaas (1987) data, and the supposed weaknesses of the study.

The weaknesses cited often center around issues of whether or not the study was valid due to concerns about randomization of subjects. To be honest, while the assignment of students into experimental and control groups was not truly random in the classic sense, it was functionally random and created equivalent groups. That is what randomization is intended to accomplish, and the Lovaas team made it happen.

What if it hadn't? What if only high-functioning students had been selected, and only the highest put into the experimental group? I would argue that the results of the study would still be fascinating. It is a classic case of losing the forest for the trees when we argue about randomization and forget that this was the first systematic demonstration of complete recovery in about one half of a sample. Show me another methodology that achieves this end and I'll discuss supposed flaws in experimental design with you all day.

I remember one Halloween in 1990 or 1991. My friend Susan Cara and I drove a couple of hours from the city up to Spring Valley, New York, to a little club where the rock performer Meat Loaf was playing. Meat Loaf had achieved great fame some 15 years earlier with his landmark album, "Bat out of Hell." This album featured lyrics by the best lyricist going, Jim Steinman, as well as production by Todd Rundgren. Combined with Meat Loaf's powerful theatrical style, this album redefined what rock music was capable of being.

So why was Meat playing such a tiny venue? Basically, it is because the public has a very short memory. This was before Meat's "comeback" in the mid 1990's, when he began to sell out large arenas again. Those of us who grew up listening to him, however, never stopped going to the shows. We weren't there because he was popular. We were there because he does the best rock concert there is, period. Legends abound of his needing oxygen at the end of his shows, with new band members terrified that he was dying and more experienced members stepping over him and saying, "Nice show."

I saw Meat in concert again last night as I write this, a sold- out show in the heart of New York City. His musical style hasn't changed. Newer albums have all the quality and breaking all the rules of "top 40" that the older ones had. His music hasn't changed, but the public has learned that songs don't have to be less than four minutes long and consist of catchy refrains. Real thought, emotion, and power can come through.

ABA is the Meat Loaf of the world of autism treatment. It has waxed and waned in popularity. Right now, like Meat Loaf, we're riding a wave of popularity. Just like Meat, we haven't changed. The world has simply changed around us, rediscovering what many of us knew all along: that ABA is the best thing going. It may not follow the conventional rules of what is supposed to be popular, but there it is. Popularity is no assurance of quality, often quite the opposite.

ABA has the power to change behavior like no other system yet developed. Still, this power does not tell us what we should work on, what we should be doing at any particular moment. Even in the world of ABA, we sometimes lose track of what we are working on and why. I see people doing dozens of discrete trial teaching programs for people with autism, forgetting why they're doing them. We must constantly ask ourselves: is there any kind of functional skill being taught here? Is this a priority skill for him to master at this point?

I found myself doing programming for a summer camp a couple of summers ago. That magic moment came when all the programs were written and being implemented. I could turn to other matters. One student was going to need to have his psychological evaluation updated next month, so I took the time to get a jump on it. This student was going to need a Creole translator, and luckily I had several qualified people among my camp staff.

Doing IQ tests for students with autism is a dubious matter at best. Most often, I try to use it as a behavior sample as much as any kind of standardized measure. What we usually get is a measure of the degree to which students have learned to focus and follow directions and imitate, as opposed to any direct measure of intelligence, whatever that is.

The test was over, and I began scoring it. An eight year old student named Alex had come into the room following the test. He had earned time to play computer games by tasting new foods he had previously refused. I set him up with some computer pinball, and showed him how to use it. I threw in some verbal sound effects, binging and pinging as he tried out the game. What do I care if I look and sound silly? It's not like I have any dignity anyway. This isn't a field to go into if you want to maintain your dignity. I've had students throw water on me as a reinforcer. So what? Do what works and then shape it into something more normalizing as you get ready to mainstream.

We each set about our appointed tasks, although I was sure Alex would have more fun than I would. Scoring IQ tests, particularly for children with autism, is about as interesting as listening to a pop singer or actress talk about the direction her career is taking. Alex, though, loved computer games. One of his classmates had summed it up: "Alex is great at the games, but he likes to play alone." It was true. He was very skilled at the computer games, but his social skills were still lagging.

As I scored the IQ test, not to my surprise, I discovered that the previous tester had derived a composite score some 30 points lower than what I derived. I guess that meant we were on the right track with our work with the student. From behind me, I heard a small voice.

"Bobby?"

"Yeah, dude?" I replied without looking up from my paperwork, figuring that he needed help with the game. It must have locked up or something.

"Can you come watch me?"

I could lie and say that I hadn't been watching him play because I really wanted him to work to get my attention, and then to reinforce the initiation. I could say that my criterion for an initiation was very high so as to build in frustration tolerance on his end and get him to keep at it. It would be a nice story, but it would be a lie. I was distracted with the bloody IQ test.

Reality smacked me in the face. I had forgotten what I was really supposed to be working on at that moment. I absolutely should have been watching him play and providing my sound effects, giving him my undivided attention. The IQ test could be scored at three in the morning, when everyone was asleep. The priority was Alex and jumping all over this opportunity to teach him how much fun social interactions could be. He wanted an audience and to share the experience of the game. Ira Cohen, a psychologist I really respect, talks about the desire to share experiences as one of the key things to look for in determining student progress. I heard Ira echoing in my head. Ira is too nice to ever lecture someone, so I silently lectured myself as I moved to Alex and the computer at mach five.

For much longer than he had originally earned, Alex and I played with the computer pinball. He racked up point after point while I made every silly pinball noise I could muster. We did high fives and cheers that sounded like mountain gorillas on acid. We even threw in a few professional football (gentle) head-butts and stomach bumps. When his counselor came back to pick him up, she saw a scene with all the energy, not to mention volume, of a Meat Loaf show. It must have been somewhat disconcerting. The joyful chaos we all felt at that moment was reminiscent of a line from one of Jim Steinman's songs, as performed by Meat: "Everything louder than everything else." Reinforcement is often like that with young children, if you're doing it right.

Chapter Nineteen: My Role as a Related Service Provider at an ABA School for Children with Autism

Meredith S. Needelman

How I Got Here

" I think that this is a good match." Those are the words that concluded my interview for a speech/language pathologist position at an ABA school for children with autism. I had no idea at the time how true that statement was. I needed a full-time position immediately. All that I remember from the advertisement was:

1) children with autism and

2) "will train."

The second phrase was what motivated me to call. I had been providing speech/language therapy for three years, but had only one experience working with children with autism. I spent three months at a private practice that followed the philosophy of Sensory Integration in the treatment of children with a variety of communication disorders, including autism. I quickly became adept at techniques such as brushing, deep pressure, and light stimulation. I swung children on swings and bounced them on balls in an attempt to obtain eye contact, identify an object, or stimulate a "b" sound. My dissatisfaction and frustration increased, however, as I was unable to document any significant progress on the part of the children. Moreover, the extensive data collection that was emphasized in my training as a speech therapist was not emphasized in this private practice. I left after that summer thinking that the autistic population was just "not for me."

I therefore thought that the interview at the ABA school for children with autism would last about five minutes. I stayed for its entirety and hung on every word. Not only did the methodology described hinge on quantitative analysis and documentation, but I was told that it worked. I felt like I had the rare and unique opportunity to join a winning team, for the first time in my career.

I defined Applied Behavior Analysis to a relative that day, and described a few of the features associated with it. She responded that this school year, if I accepted this position, would be telling. She predicted that by the end of the year, I would either fully support this methodology, or that I would disagree with it to the point that I would need to leave.

My Initial Experience

For the first few months, I was unsure. I liked that ABA had features of my training inherent in its structure. During my speech training, for example, we learned to take data on specific objectives and to strive to achieve mastery of those objectives. Within the ABA structure of this particular school, the child had to demonstrate a skill 90% of opportunities, three consecutive times, and across two different trainers, before the skill was considered mastered. At speech school, we were taught to teach new skills in a structured environment and then "transfer" those skills to other settings. The ABA world calls this generalization, a change of word but not focus. My speech training focused on learning skills in a hierarchy. For example, if a child could not produce an "r" sound, we taught it first in isolation (e.g., "Say 'er'.") Once the child was able to do that, we taught it in words, then phrases, then sentences, then in conversation. This is similar to what in ABA is called chaining, again a change in name but not in purpose or methodology. Once a child mastered a skill in isolation, that skill was paired with others already learned and put into more naturalistic and difficult contexts (randomization). Finally, my university professors taught us about the importance of reinforcement. We carried toys and games with us at all times, and became very well-versed in saying "Good job!" after every correct communicative response from the child. Reinforcement, of course, is also a critical aspect of ABA.

I also learned that ABA had features that were markedly different from my schooling in speech/language pathology. We learned in school, for example, that every skill must be introduced and modeled before teaching. We'd say, for example, "Today we are going to work on asking questions. This is important, because this helps us get things we want and need." With ABA, we proceed directly into the task without the need for an elaborate introduction.

At speech school, we were taught to reinforce prompted trials, using whatever prompts were necessary to elicit the desired response, and to reinforce approximations that were less perfect than observed previously. At this ABA school, we reinforce only the best approximation that had ever been observed, systematically using only the least intrusive prompt level that had been reached.

Finally, my university only taught me how to remediate communicative behavior. Other behaviors were not emphasized in my training. If a child "misbehaved" during my session, but continued to produce correct communication responses, I was not concerned. ABA focuses on all behaviors. If a child is acting inappropriately during a session at our school, that behavior is immediately addressed and redirected. In a typical speech session, if a child was hitting himself while speaking properly, I might still reinforce. Such a condition would be anathema to a behavior analyst.

The Study

Three months into my school year at this ABA school, I was asked to participate in a research study that would help reconcile my opinions about ABA. The study investigated the role of related services with our population of children. For my part, I was asked to select two children of pre-school age. To one child, I provided traditional speech/language therapy as I had learned and practiced for years prior to this position. I used objectives based on both the child's IEP and his estimated functioning level. I provided ABA services to the other child, strictly following the procedures as outlined in each discrete trial program.

An interesting finding in the study was that both children demonstrated progress in their communication skills. Also interesting, was that each day into the study, I found myself less able to "remember" the traditional speech method. I caught myself using the language of ABA during my traditional speech sessions. I actually ended up asking a new speech therapist at school to join in the study, as I believed that she would better be able than I to provide the "traditional" speech therapy.

The conclusions of the study, however, were unsettling. The conditions of my part, namely

1) Speech therapist providing ABA, and

2) Speech therapist providing traditional speech therapy,

were compared with the two other conditions of

3) Teachers, teaching assistants, and speech therapists providing ABA, and

4) Teachers and teaching assistants providing ABA without the help of a speech therapist.

The data demonstrated no difference between the last two conditions, suggesting little need for the speech therapist in the delivery of ABA services. In fact, conditions where the speech person worked alone led to a difficulty not seen with the other conditions. When other staff attempted to conduct the same drills that had previously been worked on only by the speech therapist, there was little or no generalization of skills to other staff members.

Why I Belong Here

What do such results say about my role as a related service provider? Initially, I was frustrated and defensive. "I am needed here because I do things differently than other staff," I said. "I am needed here, because I can do things that other classroom staff cannot do." What I now realize is that my reaction was against the whole ABA process, which ironically works precisely because all staff are *supposed* to do the same thing in the same way. The data, in my opinion, actually celebrate the ABA methodology. What I needed to do for my own peace of mind was to rationalize why my position is needed within the ABA framework. I consulted with a certified behavior analyst, various teachers, and other related service providers, and came up with an argument that reinvigorated my enthusiasm to come to work each day.

First, my position as speech/language pathologist is needed when ABA programs do not follow a standard pattern. In the programs involved in the study, the programs (e.g., object labeling, requesting, and color identification) were standard in their steps and teaching procedures. What would happen when a program did not follow a standard procedure? For example, a verbal imitation program might need to be tailored and modified to accommodate the speech production skills of a student. Only a speech therapist is qualified to administer and interpret the results of an articulation test that best determines these skills.

We are then essential to the development and implementation of the program that all staff can follow, not to mention training the staff to carry out the procedures. Another example may be the oral-motor command program. What would happen when a child is not physically able to execute the fine movements of the tongue, lips, and jaw? Speech therapists are trained to facilitate these movements, redesign the program, and train classroom staff in these areas.

Second, I feel my position is needed to facilitate receptive and expressive language skills outside of the discrete trial setting. As an expert in normal communication skills, I can teach classroom staff how to incorporate language into any and all activities in the child's school day, in several ways:

1)   I can provide group language lessons. Currently, I am coming into the classrooms daily and providing lessons based on thematic units that address basic communication abilities.

2)   I can demonstrate how to expand a child's utterances. For example, if a child produces a three word utterance, I can show classroom staff how to turn that into a longer, more complex sentence congruent with utterances typical of that child's age.

3)   I can provide teaching strategies to constantly stay on the child's cutting edge of language development. Such strategies include modeling concise and correct grammar, checking for clarification of instructions given, and incorporating sequencing and categorizing into teaching to facilitate new vocabulary. By facilitating language outside of discrete trials, I am striving to

generalize the skills acquired in that structured setting to more natural and functional contexts.

I find that I am a critical team member when specific communication disorders arise. How does a program need to be modified to address a stuttering problem? Speech therapists are well-versed in procedures to address dysfluency and incorporate these procedures into the child's programming. What happens when a child, over the course of time, becomes increasingly hoarse? Only the speech therapist is able to make the necessary referral to an ENT physician to rule out a physical etiology to the problem. In the event that a physical problem such as vocal nodules exists, speech therapists are indispensable team members to design a plan to address the physical abnormality while staying consistent to the child's behavioral programs.

Concluding Thoughts

So, how is it that I use the philosophies and methodology of Applied Behavior Analysis to carry out my duties as a speech/language pathologist? My experience this past year has led me to the same conclusion every time that I ask myself that question. As a related service provider, I feel that I can take principles from my speech and language training and integrate them into what I have learned about behavioral intervention, maintaining the integrity of both areas.

Yes, I am a speech/language pathologist. In this setting, however, I am also a behavior analyst. I am one member of a team of psychologists, teachers, teaching assistants, physical therapists, occupational therapists, and parents who are also behavior analysts. We all spend each day addressing and redirecting the inappropriate behaviors of children with autism, using the principles of behavior analysis to address socially significant behavior.

My father made a nice analogy. In a volleyball game, the players rotate their positions. Every player will be a striker or a server at one time or another. They adjust their roles to accommodate where they are standing, but they all have the same primary goal in mind: to get the ball over the net, and are all critical to that end. I am one player on a team of people whose end goal is appropriate social, adaptive, motoric, academic, and communicative behavior. With a team of experts in all of these above areas, we are well on our way to winning the game of autism recovery.

Chapter Twenty: Everyone Learns About Reinforcement
Catherine D. Sales

My story is about Eric and the struggle we had teaching him to discriminate between objects, pictures, and body parts. This is really an example of how we often learn more than our students.

Eric was a three-year-old boy at the time I started to work with him. He was little and cute in every description. Before the age of two, he was diagnosed as having autism. The medical and educational professionals observed many of the characteristics that deem such a small being as having a disability. Eric came to me with some basic attending and matching skills. He was always smiling and forever jumping around. He didn't use words, and didn't have other adaptive ways to communicate at that point. For a "non-vocal" kid, though, he sure did make a lot of noise. For the time being, he was mine for five hours a day. He worked with two teaching assistants, under my direct supervision, during that time.

Eric learned to use a modified picture exchange system to communicate. He learned the correspondence between many photo icons and used them reliably to express his needs and wants. In this manner, he was able to communicate clearly and did so frequently. We worked on eye contact and other attending skills. We concentrated on following directions, imitating actions, early communication skills, and many other behaviors during those beginning weeks and months.

Early in the school year, his parents decided to try one of the elimination diets that many therapists suggest. Given that this is not an intrusive measure and served only to eliminate junk food, we weren't opposed to this most recent effort to "fix" Eric's behavioral excesses. We used different food items to motivate him once his diet was restricted, and we taught him to use a new set of photo cards to communicate his wants. He continued to make requests with the same frequency as before the diet restrictions. He consumed the edibles from the list of "can haves" and continued to play with his puzzles, rice box, and crayons.

Eric did not tantrum or fuss when he was denied access to treats that he was previously allowed to eat. We often found him hunting through the room, however, looking for ways to steal the better snacks from the other students. No one could find a small morsel of the forbidden foods on the floor with greater accuracy and speed than Eric. He could hone in on a chipped piece of candy coating from a skittle at a distance of ten feet. It is a skill that still amazes me.

Eric knows the routine; the teacher presents a direction, he responds and then, when the teacher says, "Great job!" he requests one of his back-up reinforcers. He does this well, as he happily alternates between the sugar-free lollipops and non-dairy chocolate.

During one-to-one instructional time, Eric was following

directions, matching pictures and doing well on many different tasks. He continued to do well on all of the programs we were teaching prior to the diet changes. But, when we looked at body part identification and other new programs, we were just not making any progress. We analyzed error patterns and adjusted our instruction. The data showed that he was having specific problems pointing to foot and head, so we changed the intonation of our voice to help prompt him, but that didn't work. His imitation skills were solid, so we tried fading modeled prompts. We still saw no success. When he began to respond too quickly, we implemented a response delay. We tried several other strategies that seemed to be indicated by his behavior, but the data never showed correct responding over sixty percent. The occupational therapist suggested that it was hard for him to point/touch his own body parts, so we tried having him point on a doll. His attention to the instruction was inconsistent. I became desperate, so I brought in a three-foot doll of "Chucky" from the Rugrats (TM). I was hoping that we could get better attention from him (it certainly got the attention of the other kids in the room). We kept his parents informed of our latest "breakthrough" instructional hopes, and they also tried at home to help him with this task. I was really frustrated, but it wasn't because I didn't know what to do, it was because I knew what would work effectively and I was prevented from doing it.

One day, while observing the teacher assistant working with Eric, I found myself knowing exactly what to do. I would get

141

the correct behavior to occur once and reinforce it immediately by delivering some desired item. Of course, that sounds like what we should have been doing all along, and we thought we were. All incidental behavior indicated we were delivering reinforcers. Eric used his pictures to tell us what he wanted, he consumed what we gave him immediately, and we moved on to the next trial. Something in his behavior, though, had me saying out loud what I had been saying to myself for days, "Those carob raisins just aren't functioning as a reinforcer."

That "something" in his behavior was the chance level of correct responding to the target behavior of pointing to head and foot. So, I decided to do a quick data demonstration. I ran two sessions with Eric myself, giving him whatever he wanted. I let him point to any food item or toy we had available in the room. He wanted peanut butter cookies. I gave very small pieces; in the end he got less than two cookies over forty trials. During those two sessions, Eric performed with ninety-five percent accuracy. I then ran several sessions, denying him access to these reinforcers and the level dropped back down.

A few minutes later, his mother walked in to pick him up. I quickly graphed the data and showed it to her. She asked what we did in those two sessions. I told her and, without hesitation, she said, "If you can get him to do that, then use whatever you need to." The next day, he wasn't interested in the peanut butter cookies so we looked for something else. This is a constant campaign with him, but so it is for all students. At least we didn't feel as though our hands were tied anymore.

Eric has gone on to master that task and many others. He is now starting to vocally communicate. His rate of progress has surprised all of us. For a while, we kept track of the amount of the forbidden foods he ate. This information was given to his parents and other therapists so they could collect some anecdotal data on his jumping around.

I wish to make clear that I don't recommend that parental requests be ignored. It is very important that we work together. In this situation, I could have consulted with his parents first. I chose not to, because I felt that I had the optimal motivational conditions at that moment. It wasn't my intention to try to convince Eric's parents to dismiss the diet, although I have not seen the benefits of the diet in my experience. This proved to be an occasion where the numbers spoke for themselves. They had been talking, I just wasn't listening.

Teaching the principle of reinforcement can be a rather difficult task. The first thing to remember is that individuals are not reinforced; only behavior is reinforced. Only the effect on the behavior will tell you whether or not reinforcement has or is occurring.

If it all goes the way you plan, then it's easy to understand. If the desired behavioral outcome does not occur, however, then it is not unusual for teachers to have trouble figuring out the problem. My goal in working with parents and professionals is to teach those working with the children to attend to the kid's behavior, particularly what (s)he finds reinforcing. Now, a simple objective like that does not seem difficult, but eliminating the distractions is actually more complicated at times.

Reinforcement works, it's just a matter of finding a reinforcer. Statements like, "Reinforcement doesn't work with him," "His reinforcers don't work," "She doesn't like her reinforcers," or even, "She likes her reinforcers," simply do not make sense. Reinforcement works, you just have to find a reinforcer. Reinforcement by definition increases behavior. If the behavior does not increase, then again you do not have a reinforcer. Throwing your hands up in frustration and saying, "He just doesn't feel like doing it," or "(S)he's in a mood," means giving up the battle before it has even started. When you find yourself saying these things, you are indirectly identifying aspects of the child's instruction that are within your field of control. It's all about motivation and finding reinforcers.

Eric's learning obstacles were not completely ameliorated. There were many other challenges and his overall improvement has been due to many factors, none of which are immune to the question of reinforcement. If, at the end of this tale, what stands out is that a parent dropped her convictions to follow through on a special diet for her son, then the reader has missed the point. The point of this story is not that I convinced a parent to change her child's diet or allow us to use edibles, but rather that a parent and a teacher learned to look more closely and accurately at the child's behavior. We looked at the data. The data controlled our instructional decisions. Maybe a byline for this story is one on the importance of data collection. The student is always "right." We have to remember this at all times, and the data will tells us the next step to take.

Chapter Twenty-One: The Sunshine behind the Clouds
Gia Tarica

Even before I actually began my formal career, I was often asked by family, friends and advisors to reconsider my decision to work amongst children with complex developmental disabilities. I was told that the rate of progress, if any at all, was drastically slow and therefore it left most teachers feeling unappreciated and unfulfilled. For over two years, I've been working with children diagnosed with autistic-spectrum disorders, and I am truly grateful I wasn't swayed to take another career path. Although there is no specific cause or cure for autism, with appropriate behavioral intervention, significant results are seen. While some people diagnosed with pervasive developmental disabilities remain supervised for a large portion of their lives, data have shown that others have made sufficient progress through ABA that they are characterized as indistinguishable from the typically developing child. I taught at a school for children with autism for a year, with children aged eight to ten years old. This school utilized the principles of applied behavior analysis, and over the year I witnessed significant changes in a certain student; his name is David.

When David entered on the first day of school, he hesitantly walked into the classroom with his fingers plugging both ears. I bent down, to be at the same eye level, and introduced myself as his new teacher. He was unfazed and unresponsive to my attempt at initiating a conversation. Instead, David was completely focused on the stereo, situated in the middle of the classroom, softly playing light music. Five minutes later, his backpack was still on his back, untouched, and his two fingers were still in his ears as David stood in the corner of the classroom, glaring at the radio, expressionless. It was time to turn off the radio and learn about this child who seemed unreachable and so far away.

After the first few days of school, David displayed a few behaviors that we thought were imperative for amelioration. We took frequency data sheets, to show how many times these specific behaviors occurred throughout the day, along with A-B-C sheets (antecedent, behavior, consequence).

We first took data on David's "out of seat" behavior. During an unpreferred activity, usually a language lesson, David seemed completely disinterested, causing him to remove himself from the activity and wander the room in search of more appealing activities. After one verbal attempt at getting him back to his seat, we then walked over to him and had to physically prompt him to his chair. This process was something that involved two or three people. David was always initially noncompliant and with that, a tantrum was bound to occur. His body would stiffen so tightly that three staff members would use all of their strength to form his body to the chair. He would fight us with every bone in his body, and this kind of episode always resulted in tears.

David's receptive skills were always far stronger than his expressive communication. He had no problem following a two to three step directive, but stating his needs and wants were tremendously difficult for him. When he found himself frustrated, he would often grind his teeth, without saying a word. I always sensed that David's noncompliance and tantrums were rooted in a lack of ability to express himself - a frustration from within.

It is a common trait for autistic children to display perseverative behaviors. David perseverated on computer games, story books, music tapes and basically anything else he found enchanting. He played computer games inappropriately; unable to move to a new screen because he was so enthralled with a sentence or a movement on the previous screen. During a lesson, he would greatly amuse himself with something as simple as the pencil on his desk. He had a tendency to roll the pencil across his desk until it fell on the floor, which greatly entertained him and caused him to repeatedly perform this motion. The few sentences David spoke were accompanied by hand movements. He didn't understand the concept of speaking without his hands "speaking" simultaneously with his mouth.

Another perseveration involved feathers. If we used feathers in a lesson, he would throw them up in the air and watch them lightly float down to the surface of his desk. He was so fascinated at the sight of this that diverting his attention to the lesson was almost impossible. David wasn't concentrating or focusing on anything academic. Taking away the feather or the pencil was not the answer. We knew that at some point in his life, someone wouldn't know that they should eliminate these things from him; that he wouldn't be able to focus and concentrate with them around. Our goal was to continue exposing him to objects and have him control his urges and act as appropriately as he possibly could with the distracting stimuli present.

David was mandated to receive occupational, speech and physical therapy several times a week. He absolutely loathed the thought of missing out on the classroom activities to receive related services, and frequently tantrummed when he was taken to another part of the classroom to receive his 1 on 1. Many times his entire body had to be physically lifted, while he was screaming and crying, desperately not wanting to leave the group. He displayed the same behavior when we took him to the bathroom without being accompanied by any other class members. There were times when he was obviously holding the need to urinate because he didn't want to be taken alone without his friends. While this degree of social relatedness was indeed a strength for David, his NEEDING to have others around proved to be a roadblock in the way of his learning of independence.

Our opening strategy was to have David's mother send in several juice boxes so that he would drink so much that he couldn't possibly hold it in any longer. (He wouldn't look twice at drinking water; he thoroughly and entirely refused and this was a large concern for his parents.) Along with the goal of finding the courage to leave the classroom alone with a staff member, it was extremely important for David to initiate conversation. If he drank more liquids than his bladder could hold, we hoped he would initiate the need to go to the bathroom. As you will see, this proved to be one example of an effective intervention.

Spontaneous conversation was always a major delay for David. He never spontaneously greeted staff members or initiated any need for anything. He was notably prompt-dependent and he would only respond accurately after receiving a prompt. For example, if we were doing an art project that involved glue and scissors (and the rest of the class were outrightly utilizing the materials), David would sit in his chair and not ask for a thing until he was prompted, "Do you need a scissors?" He'd then respond, "yes." This was an ongoing struggle for David and issues we dealt with daily.

David's cognitive abilities were significantly higher than many of his classmates, but his social/emotional deficits always prevented him from learning more quickly, actively participating and expressing his knowledge. David could easily read sight words, along with stories, but had a fear of reading aloud. This, combined with his prompt-dependency, made it very difficult to know exactly how much he was processing or knew prior to the lesson. David's lack of confidence was continually delaying his learning. After reading a story, it was very difficult to know how much David had comprehended. When asked to answer "Wh" questions, he would whine and refuse to answer. When encouraged to answer, a tantrum would ensue.

The first few weeks were filled with a child we could hardly reach, an existence so untouchable and foreign to us all. Through meetings with the psychologist, master teacher, social worker, parents and other insightful minds, however, we have seen drastic changes in David's world. Utilizing the principles of applied behavior analysis, along with the persistence, love, consistency and patience of everyone surrounding David, we are slowly watching him creep out of the world where he was so concealed and hidden for so long.

We started working in very small steps with David's behavior, and, after the first few days, we realized that he responded very well to primary reinforcers and verbal praise. One of David's favorite snacks was cookies and that was the initial reinforcement we utilized. During any kind of structured activity, we had a staff member sitting behind David's chair, reinforcing every appropriate behavior. We started from the beginning, using one minute as our time frame. The staff member had her own chair directly behind David's chair, legs on either side of his, a bag of cookies in one hand, a timer in the other and a data sheet somewhere in reach. We started on David's "out of seat" behavior, and for every minute that he didn't get out of his seat, this was reinforced with a piece of a cookie and loud, dramatic praise from all the staff members ("GREAT JOB STAYING IN YOUR SEAT!"). David absolutely loved the verbal praise, along with the reinforcers, and after repeated successes, we increased the timing and faded the reinforcers (along with ourselves). After a few weeks, David was sitting through an entire lesson, without a staff member behind him. Someone looking in on the classroom now, would never know that this was ever an issue for David. He sits beautifully through every structured activity.

We used the same approach when dealing with his perseverative behaviors. During computer time, there would always be a staff member behind him, reinforcing when he appropriately moved from one screen to another. When he spoke with his hands, we all consistently used the terminology "hands down" along with reinforcing every time he didn't speak with his hands. We eventually got to the point where we could fade ourselves completely and fade out the primary reinforcement. Now, David sits nicely when he listens to music and rarely perseverates on the words, plays computer games appropriately, rarely speaks with his hands, stays in his seat and can concentrate far better than ever before. When David exhibits these behaviors again every once in a while, we can simply redirect him and see a positive result. In the past, it took much more than redirection and was always accompanied by a tantrum.

We then needed to really push David on verbally expressing himself. We decided to expose him to a preferred activity, and teach incidentally while motivation was high. For example, he had a favorite ball that he liked to bounce during movement class. We would hold the ball and not allow him to have it until he "used his words," a statement continually used with David throughout his day. At first, he just looked sad and confused as to why we weren't allowing him to play with it.

We used this method for almost everything during his day, modeling the verbal statement and not giving him the desired item until he repeated properly (or spoke independently). We'd give him his juice box without the straw, a worksheet without the pencil, crayons with no paper, lunch with no spoon. We attempted to fade our prompts whenever possible, as we wanted him to initiate conversation! We'd take him to the bathroom with the rest of the class, and everyone would ask to go inside. We wouldn't allow David until he requested to do so. We'd walk up to him and say, "David, use your words." "I want ball please," or "I want straw please," or "I want pencil please," or "I want paper please," or "I want spoon please," or "I want bathroom please." He eventually started repeating when we modeled the statement for him, and we once again reinforced every appropriate sentence with the object he desired and continuous verbal praise. Though it took months, David now spontaneously makes requests throughout the entire day. He went from being a silent child who could follow simple directions to an outgoing boy who spontaneously pokes his head in classrooms and greets friends and teachers.

His confidence with initiating has generalized to other

areas. Using the same approach, we have seen drastic improvements with all communication abilities. David now stands in front of the class and reads sight words from the board, and sentences from books. When he needs to go to the bathroom, he simply asks and usually likes to be accompanied by a certain favorite friend in the classroom (we're working on eventually fading the friend). David takes an interest in certain people, and not in others, as would a typically developing child. He is now able to see how much of life is opened for him, simply by being able to express himself. With his ability to communicate, he can tell us when he doesn't want to do something and we can discuss it together and he understands. We don't see any signs of frustration with David anymore, which has dramatically decreased his tantrums to a point where we haven't seen one in months. Through his new communicative abilities, we have influenced him to try new foods and now he even drinks water!

A major factor in David's progress has been the consistency we have seen at home. We communicate every single day with his parents regarding any concern we have and they are adamant about following through with whatever we do in school. They have been exceptional and have gone to extremes to achieve these improvements with David. Together we have watched their child blossom into his new world. We can now see the sunshine behind the clouds.

Chapter Twenty-Two: Maurice Begins to Communicate
(And Stops Tantrumming!)
Deborah L. Meinberg

The first time I met Maurice, he and his teacher were in a battle to get Maurice to sit in his chair while working. His teacher, Karen, would sit him down. He would then fall to the floor and let out a blood-curdling scream like I'd never heard before. I watched this cycle for a few moments and knew right away that this was a child I wanted to become involved with. From his quiet little voice (which oddly enough resembled that of Elmo from Sesame Street), to his loud screaming, he and his ability to dominate a situation fascinated me. I spent a lot of time with Maurice, Karen, and Tiffany (his other teacher) over the next few weeks, learning as much as I could about his skills, and what was functioning to maintain his tantrums. These tantrums would often last for at least a half hour at a time, during which no actual work was accomplished, with Maurice spending most of it on the floor and screaming. Needless to say, both of his teachers were at a loss and ready for some help.

As I got to know Maurice, I learned that he was a four-year-old student who had been attending our school for approximately six months. Having been involved with home programming during early intervention, Maurice came in with a skill set that he did not display consistently at school. Yet, through various probes, it was apparent that Maurice did actually possess a wide range of skills that he was adamant about keeping to himself. Maurice could tact (label) and discriminate numerous pictures, numbers, letters, shapes and colors. He could match and point and had even begun a pre-reading program. Maurice also manded (requested) in one word utterances for desired items. His behavior, however, was under no "instructional control." "Instructional control" is a fancy way for terming the set of skills needed to attend to a given task. Making eye contact and sitting still when told are two of the building blocks of all other skills. Maurice displayed neither of these. This was an obvious place to start. I also wanted to look at Maurice's reinforcer repertoire.

While observing Maurice and his teachers, it became apparent that finding reinforcers for Maurice was not the problem. Anything to do with Thomas the Tank Engine (TM) was good enough for him. He had Thomas books, stickers, cards, puzzles, and trains. He also had a range of edibles that at one time or another functioned as reinforcers. What surprised me, however, was that while Maurice had quite a few mands in his repertoire, he did not use them consistently. It also became apparent to me what was maintaining Maurice's tantrums: lack of access to his favorite items. If he would ask for "chip," for example, and was told to wait and that he could work for it, he would start screaming. Maurice and his teachers would then get into a verbal battle, with the teacher trying to reassure Maurice that he could actually work for the item and

Maurice screaming. I realized that it wasn't that we did not have reinforcers for Maurice, but rather that his mand repertoire had been so thickly reinforced previously that he now did not understand when he had to wait. He just simply did not understand why, if he asked for something, he couldn't always get it right then and there. Instead of using his words then, his mands took the form of screaming and he no longer asked appropriately for the things he wanted. I decided that this was my second and probably most important area of focus: teaching Maurice to communicate and to wait appropriately for his communication to be reinforced.

Once we had decided on our game plan, instructional control and mand training, we got under way. Maurice's teachers were skilled and cooperative, so working with them was not an obstacle. The first thing we did was to bombard Maurice with a "sit still" program and a "wait" program. We were teaching Maurice to respond to those two antecedents and emit the appropriate behavior for a specified amount of time (1-5 seconds) before having access to a desired item. Every instance of this behavior was reinforced immediately with the delivery of the desired item. Once these behaviors were in Maurice's repertoire (we defined this as responding correctly to either antecedent 95% of the time when dispersed throughout the day), we began to work on mand training.

By far, one of the most important skills we can teach our children is to communicate with us what it is they want. By this time, Maurice had begun to talk in phrases, so we immediately began to require Maurice to ask for desired items with a phrase ("item please").   Maurice learned new mands quickly and frequently generalized them to the natural setting within a couple of days. This was a very exciting time for both Maurice and his teachers, because as Maurice began to ask for what he wanted, his tantrums started to grow shorter. They were still marked with loud screaming and falling to the floor, but Maurice began to respond to the "sit still" command during these difficult times. We also started to generalize "wait" by saying "wait" right after Maurice manded, having him wait for one second and then delivering the item. This was teaching Maurice to handle a bit of latency between the request and delivery of that item. This was difficult, seeing as Maurice would pretty much do flips if he could for a Thomas the Tank Engine toy. Waiting was a long and arduous road.

During this time, I was also working with the teachers to decrease the amount of extraneous verbalizations they engaged in with Maurice. While vocal interactions were both appropriate and welcome during play times and praise situations, there were times when talking to Maurice too much would exacerbate the situation. For example, if Maurice would ask for something as the teacher was about to present an antecedent, they would often say something to the effect of, "Ok, you need to work for it. Ok get ready - just one more, here we go . . ." You get the idea. All the talking usually set off Maurice and wasted time. As we all know, the first step to changing student behavior is changing teacher behavior. Therefore, I taught the teachers to respond in one of two ways when Maurice manded at a time when delivering a tangible was unlikely. First, as Maurice's behavior was coming under the control of antecedents such as "wait" and "sit still," we should use that to our advantage. When Maurice manded and the teachers were not going to deliver, they should simply say, "wait" and immediately deliver the next antecedent. This decreased the latency between antecedents, thus giving Maurice less down time, as well as decreasing the amount of time until the next opportunity to mand. The other alternative I posed to the teachers was to simply ignore any mands Maurice emitted during these times and again, immediately deliver the next antecedent.

All went well for a few weeks. Maurice's teachers were doing a phenomenal job managing their own behavior, and in turn, the duration of Maurice's tantrums decreased, and the consistency with which he used vocal verbal behavior increased. Maurice was manding more frequently and consistently and had even begun to say a couple of full sentences with verbal prompts (such as "I want ____ please"). Maurice's behavior, however, began to plateau. We noticed that while the duration of Maurice's tantrums decreased, the frequency had not, and data reflected that they were actually increasing. Transition times had also become an increasing problem for Maurice, especially during group activities. When one activity, such as playing with legos, finished and another activity (e.g., looking at books) began, Maurice threw a tantrum.

During one such instance that was particularly difficult, I was assisting Tiffany with Maurice. The goal was to have Maurice sit in his chair for a few seconds and then engage in the target activity (on this day it was listening to a story) for a full minute before he could go home. After about 10 minutes, Maurice looked Tiffany and myself dead in the eyes and yelled, clear as a bell - "I WANT TO GO PLAY PLEASE!" He then sat down in his chair and looked up at us as if to say, "Well, are you going to let me go or what?" It was as if a light bulb had gone off and he realized that all he had to do to get his way was to sit nicely in his chair and ask for what he wanted. Maurice did listen to the story, and he did get to go play that day.

From that day on, Maurice's behavior changed. He was talking, sitting and doing his work for longer periods of time. We saw an increase in the variety and spontaneity of Maurice's vocalizations. Perhaps the pinnacle came one day when Maurice's teachers and I watched with pride and pleasure as he asked, "I want blue candy please" and pretended to feed it to a Thomas train.

Chapter Twenty-Three: Would You Like to Meet Owen?
Kathy Savino and Tara Donnellan

It can be difficult for anyone to deal with transitions, but through our experience working with children with autistic-spectrum disorders, we have found it especially difficult for this population. We are going to talk about our experience dealing with one specific child.

When we first met Owen, he had a great deal of difficulty dealing with transitions, especially those involving changes in activity or routine. During times of transition he would tantrum. These tantrums would include behaviors such as screaming, crying, stamping, and throwing his body on the floor, and on a number of occasions he would become aggressive towards others. We tried a number of approaches to extinguish these behaviors. What we found to be most effective was to ignore Owen's inappropriate behavior and engage him in another activity. When Owen was able to stop tantrumming and pull himself together, we reinforced his appropriate play with verbal praise. At times even when Owen would calm himself down, something else would set him off and the tantrums would start all over again. Sometimes Owen's tantrums were short, only lasting a few minutes. Other times his tantrums were much more severe and could last up to forty-five minutes. In addition, because the transitions occur throughout the day, it was difficult to predict which transitions were bothersome to Owen and which were not. To make matters worse, Owen's limited expressive language prevented us from determining the specific cause of the tantrum each time it happened. It was not until he was calm that we were able to prompt him to express himself. In this chapter, we are going to discuss a few behaviors that Owen exhibited and the approaches we used to deal with his behaviors.

Every day, we meet the children on the bus and accompany them into the classroom. We usually walk directly to the classroom with no detours. The first thing we do upon entering the classroom is prompt the students to unpack. One day, instead of going right to the classroom, we stopped in the main office. When Owen realized that we were deviating from the normal routine, he started to tantrum. He resisted entering the office, by refusing to walk. He also began to cry and scream. Since Owen's language is limited, it was difficult for us to figure out the reason for his tantrumming. With every second, Owen's tantrum grew worse. He became louder and began pointing to the hallway where our classroom was located. First, we tried to verbally reassure him that we eventually were going to class. When that was ineffective, we ignored the behavior and physically prompted Owen to enter the office. He continued to tantrum. This was very difficult for both Owen and for us, and very disruptive to the staff working in the office. Everyone wanted to know why this child was so upset. This drew more attention to him, making it harder for us to ignore his behavior.

While it would have been easier to have given in to Owen, this would have only reinforced his negative behavior. The screaming and crying continued throughout the time spent in the office. At this point, we realized that Owen had difficulty handling transitions. We tried to flood him with transition situations, with the hopes of decreasing the behavior by desensitizing him to the anxiety-provoking situations.

One day, we were taking our students on a tour around the school delivering holiday cards. In the first room we visited, we handed the card to the adult in the room and stayed for a few minutes to wish the children a happy holiday season. Owen and his classmates sat down for a few minutes. When it was time to leave, Owen began to cry and scream. Owen needed one-on-one assistance to leave the room because he refused to walk. He continued to scream as we walked down the hall, constantly pointing back towards the classroom we left. We then continued on, visiting other classrooms. Every time we entered and left a room the tantrums would begin again. We chose to ignore Owen's behavior, because we did not want to reinforce it. While walking back to our classroom, his tantrums escalated to the point where he sat on the floor, stamping his feet. The behavior continued into our classroom until we were able to engage him in another activity. Once he calmed down, we praised him for pulling himself together and continued with our normal schedule.

At the beginning of the day, we list our daily schedule on

the board. One day we had art, or at least we thought we had art. We had snack early and put on the children's smocks. We proceeded on to the art room. At this moment, another teacher was on her way to art with her class. We then realized that it wasn't our scheduled day for art. We turned around and went back to our classroom. This is when Owen began to throw a tantrum. He was screaming, crying, and stamping his feet. He began to yell "art" and pointed to the art room. We tried at first to explain to all of the children that we didn't have art, but were going to have gym. Owen continued his tantrum. We physically prompted him to walk back to our classroom, while we ignored the behavior. When we returned to the classroom, we began to take the children's smocks off. As we assisted Owen in the removal of his smock, he became aggressive and started to grab the teacher's arm. Again, we engaged Owen in another activity. We sat him down on the carpet and physically prompted him to complete a puzzle. He eventually calmed himself down. When he was calm, we praised him by giving him a highly desired reinforcer. For Owen, this was clapping, singing, tickling, and even dancing.

We found that ignoring the behavior while it was occurring and engaging him in another activity proved to be the most successful approach for dealing with this specific behavior. At times, this was difficult because the tantrums were loud and disruptive to the other students. In addition, when others would get involved with trying to help Owen, the extra attention only served to prolong his tantrums. Towards the end of the school year, the tantrums occurred less often and at times, he was able to independently control himself. What makes this behavior so challenging is that we cannot completely control our environment. In order to desensitize Owen, we tried to set up a variety of unexpected situations. This approach proved to be successful. While we have observed great progress, our ultimate goal is to have him independently deal with the changes that may occur in our daily routines.

Chapter Twenty-Four: The Gift of a Birthday
Siobhan Beckett

Tim was a five-year old boy with Asperger's Syndrome. He was cognitively able to complete schoolwork that was appropriate for his age, but his social skills were significantly lagging. A home-based teacher worked with Tim after school, implementing behavioral strategies to assist Tim in learning how to cope with various social situations.

Tim was approaching his sixth birthday. This is usually a very exciting time for children. They eagerly anticipate presents, friends, a junk food allowance that is greater than usual, and, most of all, being the center of attention. Tim however, was not looking forward to his birthday. He quite openly displayed his disapproval by screaming "No Birthday!" anytime the topic was discussed.

What was the problem?

Tim found the very things that usually made birthdays so exciting to be quite aversive. He did not like crowds of people, loud noise from singing, clapping, or shrieking children, nor did he enjoy junk food (especially sweets). This presented quite a dilemma. How could one encourage participation in celebrating his birthday, or family birthdays, or even encourage him to participate in his friends' birthdays? Furthermore, birthdays come only once a year, so it is a difficult celebration to "get used to." The opportunity to be exposed to a birthday, especially when you vehemently dislike them, becomes limited.

One of the first strategies was to expose Tim to various environments where there were many children and crowds. He had been taught various strategies to help him cope with these situations, in order to help him to slowly desensitize. Activities such as sporting events (swimming, judo, and baseball) and playgroups had given Tim the exposure he needed to cope with noise and crowds. His classroom environment had also prepared Tim by exposing him to a variety of events that challenged him to use and practice his coping strategies. There remained however, something that prevented Tim from enjoying the total birthday experience. He would scream, yell and cry out "No birthday!" whenever the cake with candles was presented and the traditional "Birthday Song" was sung.

Approaching the situation from a behavioral standpoint, it was decided that an approach involving the increase of incompatible behaviors might work. What was needed was to find some behavior that was incompatible with screaming and/or yelling and to reinforce that behavior. A list was made of such behaviors that would be appropriate to the situation. Laughing and blowing out the candles were incompatible with yelling and screaming, but a catalyst was needed in order to distract Tim so that he would find the birthday situation "funny."

It was decided that joke party candles would be used. Once lit, these would resist efforts to blow them out. It was hoped that Tim would become distracted by the stubborn flame while attempting to blow the candle(s) out, and therefore not concentrate on yelling or screaming during the song.

Preparation to use the candles occurred as follows: First the candles were bought and tested. It would take at least seven attempts to blow out the candle. Next, a batch of cupcakes were made that would last a week and were stored. Next, Tim was tested with the candle. A cupcake was presented to him with a lit candle on top. Fortunately, Tim was enthralled. He huffed and puffed, laughed and tried again and again. It was determined that the idea was sound. We would practice having a "birthday," using these candles to divert his attention from the aspects of the situation that typically elicited screaming. Tim's family (his parents and older brother, as well as his home-based teacher) each agreed to be the recipient of a birthday. Tim would have practice with behaving appropriately when the cake and candles were presented and the song was sung. Tim could do one of two things: enjoy the "birthday" and help blow out the candle if he was acting appropriately (no screaming or yelling), or leave the room and not participate.

The very first evening this intervention was used, Tim was unable to participate in blowing out the candle. He had worked very well in anticipation of the candle event, yet when the candle was lit and the Happy Birthday song was sung, Tim yelled out "No Birthday!" Immediately, the home-based teacher removed Tim to the basement, and proceeded to wait until the yelling ceased. Tim continued to yell, exclaiming that he wished to join everyone upstairs. His yelling was ignored until he became quiet; it was then explained that he could only return upstairs to blow out the candle if he used a "quiet voice." Tim yelled again, and again this was ignored. When the yelling ceased, he was asked if he was ready to go upstairs. He exclaimed "No" in a loud voice. The teacher continued to ignore the yelling and would turn away from Tim as he tried to yell in her direction, making his pleas. Tim continued to tantrum for approximately 30 minutes, exclaiming that he wanted to join everyone upstairs. The teacher remained quiet until the yelling stopped. She reiterated that he needed to use an appropriate voice level or the candle would be put away until the next day. Tim started to yell, "Let me blow the candle out!" She continued to ignore his wishes until the yelling stopped. When asked if he was ready to go back upstairs, Tim answered in a quiet voice, "yes." He received verbal praise for answering in an appropriate voice and they proceeded to leave the basement. Tim looked for the candle, but it had been extinguished and put away, as explained previously. He was asked why the candle was put away and he replied, " 'cause I yelled." Tim was told he could try again the next day.

On the second day, Tim had successfully completed his homework and when asked, "What are you working for?" answered, "The candle." The cupcake was taken out. A second person was selected to be the recipient of the birthday song but, this time, before the candle was lit, Tim was reminded that if he yelled he would have to leave the group. Everyone proceeded to sing the birthday song. Tim remained quiet. He attempted to blow the candle out before the song had finished and was verbally prompted to remain seated until the song was complete. Once the song was finished, Tim excitedly joined in with blowing out the candle and everyone praised him for helping with the candle. These same procedures were carried out for the remainder of the week until it was Tim's real birthday.

Tim had two tests approaching by the end of the week. The classroom was going to have a birthday party for Tim on Friday, and his real birthday was going to be celebrated on Saturday. It was decided that cupcakes would be taken to school and the same procedure would be followed there. Tim would have the candle taken away from him if he started to yell/scream. Again, Tim was given a reminder to remain quiet during the song, before the candle was lit. He was aware of the consequences and was working towards keeping the candle. Tim was remarkable! This was the first time he had sat through a group birthday party since he was 2 years of age.

When Saturday arrived, the intervention was changed. Because Tim had responded so well to the "practice" birthdays, it was decided to try generalizing his skill. A real birthday cake was going to be used, with real candles. Tim would receive the joke candle in his piece of cake while everyone else ate, provided he sat quietly through the Birthday song. Attending the party would be seven extended family members, as well as his immediate family, making a total of fifteen people who were celebrating with Tim.

At the end of the meal, the real cake and candles were presented and the singing commenced. At one point, Tim covered his ears with his hands, but one look from his mother and he put them down again. One by one, the words of the song passed until finally the last words " ...to you!" were sung. Immediately, Tim's piece of cake was cut and his special candle was lit. He received a big hug and kiss from his mother, as well as many accolades from the family members. It was a beautiful day. Tim's mother was able to witness her son enjoy his birthday, just as any other little boy would. This was a true gift!

Chapter Twenty Five: Jimmy Joins his Class
Vanetta LaRosa

Jimmy changed my understanding of children with autism. When I saw the angelic five year-old redheaded boy singing the old blues song, "Nobody knows the trouble I've seen," with woe in his voice and sadness on his face, I was hooked. From that day on, I wanted to see him excel. I was committed to helping this boy live to his fullest potential, as I was to all the children. But Jimmy was special. He was a very bright, loving, gentle-hearted soul that seemed trapped by his autism.   He wanted desperately to be a little boy, just a little boy and not a boy with autism.   There were times during our work together that he would spontaneously spit out an adult joke or an adorable child-like response. He would make fun of my over-emotional tendencies with the greatest of love by mimicking my behavior and even replicating my voice. He provided me with laughs and joy that far exceeded the compensation from the salary I received for my work with him.

I saw Jimmy as the little boy he tried to be: a boy dressed in his favorite sport's team clothing, playing with dinosaurs, needing his parents and others to love him. That is why it was especially difficult for me when he made academic progress almost beyond his grade level, but struggled terribly with socialization skills. Why couldn't he show to others what he had shown to me?   Why couldn't those fleeting moments of spontaneous behavior become everlasting? I did not know, but I vowed to try to understand what he needed to express himself.

Being relatively new in the field of autism, I learned as much as I could as fast as I could. I was fortunate to cross paths with an expert in the field that became my mentor. Dr. Bobby Newman shared his insights and knowledge with me, and, after a while, I was working as an Applied Behavior Specialist at a school set up for children with autism. I continued to work with Jimmy as his home therapist. His academic progress was incredible. By the second grade, he had met academic standards that all second graders were expected to meet. It was then that Jimmy began exhibiting bizarre repetitive behaviors. His repertoire was replete with fine stereotypic movements, such things as twirling his fingers in front of his face and licking his palms until his lips became raw.

By this time, I was well versed in behavior analytic methods and had implemented several successful behavioral programs. Jimmy had me confused, however. His regression was painful for me on a personal level. I knew I was over my head because my personal love for Jimmy was interfering with my professional responsibilities. I decided to take some time away from home programming to finish my Master's degree.

I never stopped thinking about Jimmy, though. I made sure he had qualified and caring home therapists before I took my break, but I could not stay away long. A month and a half later, I decided to see if Jimmy's parents still needed my assistance. As I always had a special relationship with Jimmy and seemed to provide him with useful therapy, his parents were thrilled to have me back. For the first time in my professional career, I had to make a conscious decision to separate my personal feelings and act professionally to help this child. This was always instinctual with everyone else.

Jimmy's behavior was spinning out of control. He would not socialize with other kids, was hiding under the table, engaging in self-stimulation to the exclusion of all other activities, and his palm licking had never ceased. He had frequent band-aids and ointment on his mouth.

The first behavior I targeted to decrease was social withdrawal. This occurred mainly at school, where he would go under the table so as not to interact in group activities. Even his academic progress was suffering, as many lessons were completed in groups. I got lucky. I was aware of Jimmy's affection for me, so I used it to reach him. I relied upon a group reinforcement technique where I provided all children who participated in the group with social attention. Social attention certainly cannot compare to M&M's (TM), but coming from me it meant something more to Jimmy. As I showered the other kids with tickles, hugs and games, it killed me to ignore Jimmy. He would peep his little red head out from under the table ever so often and grin adoringly at me. It was obvious he had a bit of a crush. I was firm and looked in the other direction. The teachers and aides were instructed to do the same. I explained to them that consistency was the key. All professionals involved had to hold firm to the behavior analytic principles. After eleven torturous days, Jimmy came out from under the table and joined his group once again as the star pupil. I don't believe he was ever showered with as much attention and love (except by his parents!). Problem #1 solved!

Next, his palm licking. Wow! How would I tackle this one? What was maintaining this behavior? Attention? Escape? Internal reinforcement? Even after conducting a functional analysis, we were not convinced. It became evident that attention and escape were not relevant factors. Intrinsic motivation was believed to be the maintaining variable. Great! That could be just about anything. Did the band-aid feel good on his skin? Did his tongue feel good against his hand? Did he like the salty taste? Or, was he just compelled to lick his palm due to obsessive thoughts? The specific reason Jimmy chose palm licking might never be discovered, so I attempted to re-direct him to a more socially acceptable behavior.

The first thing I thought was that if Jimmy were using his hands for other tasks, he would have less opportunity to lick his palms (Differential Reinforcement of Incompatible Behavior, D.R.I.). I encouraged his parents to purchase various games/toys where he could use his hands, but palm licking was still the preferred activity.

The next step was to pair a particular game with an external reinforcer to increase its potency. I chose the game of jacks so Jimmy would use his hands, concentrate, and improve fine motor skills all at once. I paired game-playing with social praise and provided the two after any appropriate behavior he displayed in the classroom. He came to view playing jacks as a gift from God. It also helped that the other kids were practically trampling each other to get in line to play. Jimmy is a social child, and the natural consequences took over. Palm licking decreased during the times he played jacks, but still existed. Fortunately, he no longer licked until his lip was raw. This behavior decreased in frequency until it disappeared and self-stimulation took another form, as it possibly always will. We will continue to shape it into more appropriate forms as it does, however.

When behavior is maintained by internal forces it may be impossible to understand the specific driving force. In general, it is best to find behaviors for clients to engage in that provide them with an equivalent internal stimulation. It is always a good idea to have items around that provide general sensory stimulation. Things like vibrating pillows, scented oils, toys that light up/vibrate, etc. It is also important to be sure that the child does not use the toy/item for self-stimulation to the exclusion of all other tasks. It is smart to ration the amount of time spent with such items and watch the individual's reaction to them.

Each behavior has its own set of variables that are responsible for its maintenance. Many behaviors stem from a complex interactions of variables. Therefore, trial and error is a part of changing many behaviors. My point is that you shouldn't be afraid to try new things. Brainstorm and you never know what will actually work. When you come to understand basic behavior analytic principles, you will be empowered to help your child, pupil, or friend achieve their greatest potential.

Epilogue: It's a Science, but it is also a Lifestyle
Bobby Newman

Although Dana and I are both Unitarian Universalists, by lineage I am descended from the orthodox Jews who fled from Eastern Europe during the early part of the 20th century, fleeing from oppression in what was then Russia and Poland. My wife's family is Catholic, from Italy. A popular true story in my family deals with when I told my mom I was going to marry Dana. Her very first words: "It's a good thing your grandfather is dead!"

I live in a sickeningly sweet world that is generally only found in the story books. My wife and mother and mother-in-law go shopping together and are happy to spend hours playing cards together and laughing about things I'm not privy to. The dads watch football together. The families get along so well that you could throw up. God forbid I ever have a disagreement with Dana. I know my mom is on her side, regardless of the actual discussion in question.

Another popular story in the family, this one not so true, is that Dana only married me so that she could have eight days of Chanukah presents in addition to Christmas. At least I hope it's not true. Anyway, we do have holiday celebrations and rituals, one on Christmas Eve that I particularly like. We all get together at my parents-in-laws' place and watch <u>The Fourth Wise Man</u>, a screen adaptation of Henry van Dyke's "The Story of the Other Wise Man." In an awesome display of dramatic talent, Martin Sheen plays Artaban, a Magi who starts out seeking the newly born Jesus to give him precious gifts. Artaban gets waylaid during his search, however. He uses the precious gifts to ransom prisoners, feed the hungry, and care for the sick. He lives his life caring for those in a leper colony, eventually becoming old and on the verge of death himself. Alan Arkin plays his long-suffering servant who resists the effort for years, only to realize at his moment of decision that his calling is to do what he has been doing all along, albeit somewhat unwillingly.

The climactic scene of the movie takes place on the first Easter Sunday. Artaban is dying. Jesus appears to him, and Artaban begs forgiveness for not having gifts to give. Jesus replies with dialogue taken from the Gospel of Matthew, 25 (35-40). Jesus says that he received the gifts, that Artaban clothed him when he was naked, fed him when he was hungry, gave him drink when he was thirsty, and took him in when he was homeless. Artaban does not understand, saying that he just met his messiah at that very moment and could not have done any of these things. Jesus replies, "As ye have done it unto one of the least of my brethren, ye have done it unto me." Artaban dies, content that his life's mission has been successfully completed. God has seen his life's work, and approved.

When I tell people that I work with people with autism, they frequently show awed reactions and say, "You must be such a wonderful, caring and patient person." Anyone who actually knows me and hears this conversation generally has to stifle a laugh. Sometimes they succeed, sometimes not. In extreme cases, continence becomes an issue. OK, so I'm not Mother Theresa. I also don't think of people with autism as the least of my brethren. They just have some behavior problems we need to work out. It's not like they're singers, actors, or athletes who actually think they deserve those millions of dollars. That's a REAL problem.

Then there's the flip-side to this "patience and caring" issue. Some people think of ABA as just a science, and think that it can be carried out by properly programmed robots. These people think of ABA as a heartless discipline, where efficiency replaces caring as a guiding force. Sorry, you lose too much skin on your hands and forearms in the early stages of work to make this argument work. If all people in this field cared about was efficiency, they'd change behavior in laboratory settings instead of in schools and hospitals.

I find myself thinking of one of the authors of a chapter you just finished reading. At the time of this occurrence, she was a Psych101 student of mine. She was working under my supervision at an afterschool program for people with autism, her first applied gig. One of her charges, a student who had just joined us that month, developed a massive nosebleed, and it took the two of us a few minutes to get it under control. This student would be described as extremely low-functioning, in his teen years and non-verbal. He had no interactive or self-help skills to speak of and engaged in self-injurious behavior by viciously biting his own foot.

When we finished with the nosebleed, we returned him to his classroom and went to wash ourselves up. Our blood-soaked shirts and gloved hands made it look like we worked in a slaughterhouse rather than a school. Suddenly, my colleague got very quiet, leaned over the sink, and burst into hysterical crying. I asked what was wrong and she replied through her tears, "He can't do *anything*!" All I could do was put a hand on her shoulder and say "Yeah." At that point in the young man's development, there was no denying it. Left alone in an apartment, he would starve to death. He couldn't even operate a can opener yet. Saying anything other than "yeah" would have been patronizing, not to mention stupid.

So where is the truth? Are people in ABA heartless technicians, or do you have to be one of the universe's anointed in order to work in the field? I think the truth is somewhere in the middle. To use an expression that I throw at Dana whenever I don't want to stop and ask directions when driving, "The journey is the thing." The very Zen message: life is the journey, not the destination. I've spent years working in this field, working alongside people who make very little money for the effort they put out. The behavior analyst in me tells me that there must be a reinforcer in there somewhere. I think the journey truly is the thing. We teach the people with autism, and they teach us as well. Reality cannot be avoided as you work within this discipline; it brings you face to face with yourself on a very deep level. If the life unconsidered is not worth living, direct care workers in ABA live a life constantly considered. You must constantly consider the lives of others, and in so doing you must consider your own.

At the end of life's journey, an account must be given of your actions. This account must be given to yourself if to no one else. As our Australian brothers and sisters would say, my co-authors have no worries. Their ledgers will be enviable.

As I was thinking of how to end this volume, it occurred to me that the people in this field share a dream, a dream about helping people to overcome the most crippling of behavioral disorders. The words of the great Jim Henson, in his persona of Kermit the Frog in The Muppet Movie, came to me:

"Yeah, well I've got a dream, too. . . . the kind of dream that gets better the more people you share it with. And I found a whole bunch of friends who have the same dream. And that makes us kind of like a family."

I can't improve on that, so I'll end it there.

About the Authors

Siobhan Beckett has been working as a Special Education Teacher in New York since 1994. She has been a home-based and Center-Based teacher with children who have been diagnosed with Autism and Asperger's Syndrome, between the ages of 18 months to six years of age. Originally from Canada, she and her family currently reside in Brooklyn, New York.

Helen Bloomer is the founder and Executive Director of Crossroads Center for Children, located in Glenville, New York, a private ABA preschool. Previously, Ms. Bloomer was trained and affiliated for ten years at the Children's Unit for Treatment and Evaluation at SUNY Binghamton under the direction of Dr. Raymond Romanczyk. Ms. Bloomer has done extensive work in the field of autism and ABA, co-authoring and presenting at numerous conferences throughout the United States. She has consulted and trained numerous school districts and private agencies in techniques of applied behavior analysis. Helen has been a member of the executive board for the New York State Association for Behavior Analysis for four years. Ms. Bloomer was a peer reviewer for New York State Department of Health clinical practice guidelines for autism/pervasive developmental disorders.

Scott Campbell received his Bachelor's and Master's degrees in Speech-Language Pathology at Loyola College in Maryland. He worked in geriatrics for three years in New Jersey, and then moved to New York and has been working with children with autism for the past two years. He is scheduled to begin research on the efficacy of speech and language assessments in preschoolers with autism.

Tara Donnellan was a teaching assistant for the Gateway Program in Oceanside, New York, and is starting a new job as a regular-education teacher. Tara is a certified elementary education teacher, working towards her Master's in special education. She also does in-home programming for children with autism, and looks forward to continuing to work with this population.

Dina Douglass is a behavioral supervisor for TheraCare. She has been a teacher in special education settings for the past nine years. She received her BA in psychology from the College of Staten Island and is planning to pursue a Master's in Behavior Analysis at Queens College. Additionally, she earned a certificate in American Sign Language interpretation at the Seymour Joseph Institute of American Sign Language. Dina has also presented empirical research at New York State Association for Behavior Analysis and Association for Behavior Analysis conferences.

Kari Ann Dunlop started in the ABA field at the Association in Manhattan for Autistic Children, but moved back upstate after a short while (city life isn't for her!). She is currently a Programming Teacher for the Crossroads Center for Children in Glenville, New York. Her duties include writing goal plans and implementing goals in discrete trial settings. She is directly involved in the analysis of the data and making changes as needed for the students. She is also pursuing a Master's degree in Special Education from Sage Graduate School in Troy, New York. She plans on becoming a certified behavior analyst when she has earned her Master's. One of Kari Ann's favorite winter activities is Ski for Light, a program where visually impaired or blind cross-country skiers are paired with sighted guides.

Amy Eisenberg received her degree as a Teacher of the Speech and Hearing Handicapped from SUNY Cortland, and is currently working on her Master's degree, with a specialty in autism, from CW Post at Long Island University. She completed an internship with the government of Mexico, and has a bilingual extension. Amy is currently a supervisor of ABA Early Intervention and SEIT services for TheraCare.

Odeisa Hichez has been working as a Teacher Assistant at the preschool of the Association in Manhattan for Autistic Children for the past three years. She received a B.A. in Psychology from the Technological Institute of Santo Domingo, in the Dominican Republic. Currently, she is pursuing her second B.A. in Biology at Hunter College of the City University of New York.

Randy Horowitz is the Director of Educational Services at the Genesis School. She received her Master's in Special Education from Queens College and her Staff Development/ Special Education Certificate in School Administration and Supervision from the college of New Rochelle. She has worked in the field of autism for over 10 years. Her clinical interests focus on educating children with autism in classroom settings. She has consulted with numerous families and programs for children with autism. In addition, Randy has presented at local, national and international conferences and workshops on topics relating to educating children with autism and related disorders.

Deborah L. Kochman, MPT, has been working at the Association in Manhattan for Autistic Children (AMAC) since March of 1999. At AMAC, Deborah has been working with children between the ages of 3 and 11, improving their gross motor skills and strengthening them physically. Together with the staff of AMAC, Deborah's ultimate goal is to enable children with autism to reach their full potential. Deborah received her Master's degree in Physical Therapy from Mercy College in July 1998 and her Bachelor's degree from Hunter College in January 1992 (Cum Laude). She is New York State licensed in Physical Therapy and a member of the American Physical Therapy Association (APTA).

Vanetta LaRosa is currently finishing her Ph.D. in psychology. During her undergraduate and graduate career, Vanetta worked extensively with children with autism, as well as individuals with a variety of severe sensory disabilities. Vanetta plans on continuing her work with these populations as she finishes her Ph.D. and pursues certification as a behavior analyst. Currently, Vanetta provides counseling and conducts evaluations for individuals with developmental disabilities.

Tami Lavie is a preschool teacher at the Association in Manhattan for Autistic Children and is currently pursuing an advanced certification in Applied Behavior Analysis at Queens College of the City University of New York. She has worked as a teacher for preschool age students with autism for the past several years. Following graduation, Tami plans on returning to her native Israel and to continue providing ABA services to children with autism.

Deborah Meinberg is a behavior analyst teaching at the Fred S. Keller School in Yonkers, New York. She recently completed her role as Interim Program Director of the David Gregory School's 1:1 Program where she had the opportunity to both supervise and teach. Deborah received a Master's degree in Applied Behavior Analysis/Behavior Disorders from Teacher's College, Columbia University in May of 1998, and is a Certified Special Education Teacher as well as a Board Certified Behavior Analyst. Deborah absolutely loves being a teacher and looks forward teaching the toddler classroom at the Keller School this fall. Deborah has a love for animals and has two cats. Her other interests include spending time with her loved ones, staying in shape, and a love of penguins.

Meredith Needelman is a speech/language pathologist currently working at the Association in Manhattan for Autistic Children. She earned a Bachelor's of Science degree in speech/language pathology at Northwestern University, and her Master's of Science degree at the University of Arizona. Her experience includes the diagnosis and treatment of a variety of communication disorders, including aphasia, dysphagia, phonological disorders, and specific language impairment. She spent four years working in the Arizona public schools. In between school years, she has worked in various private practices and a skilled nursing facility. This is her first publication.

Bobby Newman, Ph.D., C.B.A., is a licensed psychologist and Certified Behavior Analyst. Affectionately known as the Dark Overlord of ABA, his past books include Prometheus Books' The Reluctant Alliance: Behaviorism and Humanism and Dove and Orca's No Virtue in Accident and When Everybody Cares. He hosted WEVD AM's When Everybody Cares radio program. Bobby is currently the President-elect of the New York State Association for Behavior Analysis and is the Director of Quality Assurance for the Association in Manhattan for Autistic Children.

Laura M. Pajot attended St. John's University and received a Bachelor's Degree in Psychology in 1993. Her Master's Degree in Elementary Education and Special Education was completed in 1996 at Hofstra University. Her experience includes two years as a teacher's assistant and four years as an ABA classroom teacher. She is currently an independent contractor and family trainer for families of children with autism.

Josephine Parent is a mother of two children with autistic-spectrum disorders. She works as an advocate for children and families with autism, as well as applied behavior analysis.

Dana Reinecke is a Board Certified Associate Behavior Analyst. She has made numerous presentations at national conferences, and has published several articles on behavioral instruction. She co-authored a distance-learning course on behavioral methods of animal training, and is pursuing her Ph.D. at the famous Learning Processes program of Queens College. She works as a consultant in school districts, private schools, and in-home programs for children with autism.

Adrienne Robek is currently a doctoral student in the Learning Processes program in Psychology at the CUNY graduate center. She has spent the last three years conducting research on autism and working with children with autism.

Catherine D. Sales earned an Ed.D. degree in 1998 from Teachers College of Columbia University, where she also received her Master's of Education degree. She has worked at the Fred S. Keller School since 1988, where she is currently the Special Education Itinerant Teacher Services & Related Services Program Coordinator. She is a popular presenter at national and international conventions, particularly in the areas of verbal behavior, curriculum design, and teacher training. She is a Board Certified Behavior Analyst.

Kathy Savino was a teaching assistant for the Gateway Program in Oceanside, New York, and is the teacher for the new Gateway class in Merrick. She is a certified special education teacher attending graduate school to complete her Master's in reading. She also does home programming for children with autism, and looks forward to continuing this work.

Randi M. Scheiner is a registered and licensed occupational therapist who earned a Bachelor of Arts in Government from Skidmore College and a Master of Science in Occupational Therapy from Boston University's Sargent College of Allied Health Professions. Since July 1997, she has worked as an occupational therapist for children with Autistic Spectrum Disorders, learning disabilities, and emotional disturbances at the Association in Manhattan for Autistic Children. Prior to that, she worked for 2 ½ years in a hospital in Manhattan as a Senior Occupational Therapist for people of all ages with a variety of physical and neurological disabilities.

Heathyr Sheehan is a Special Education teacher in New York. She teaches elementary school-aged children with autism as the head teacher of the Oceanside branch of the Gateway program (a program for transitioning students with autism back into mainstream education). She is completing her graduate studies in Reading Education at Adelphi University in Garden City. She is a member of the International Honor Society in Education, and made her first presentation of data at the 1999 convention of the international Association for Behavior Analysis. She plans to continue her work with behavioral interventions for children with autism while pursuing certification as a Behavior Analyst.

Gia Tarica was born in Johannesberg, South Africa and immigrated to the United States in 1978. Gia graduated, with honors, from Northeastern University with a Bachelor of Science degree. She interned at The Learning and Cognitive Development Center and Perkins School for the Blind in Boston, MA, which led her along the career path to working with children with autism. She taught at the Association in Manhattan for Autistic Children and is currently pursuing a Master's degree at Hunter College for Special Education.

Sharon Toledo is a special education teacher for children with autism. She is currently pursuing a Master's degree in special education at Adelphi University. Sharon has made numerous presentations on her empirical research, and has been a guest lecturer describing how to set up ABA classrooms.

References

Alvin, J. (1976). <u>Music for the handicapped child</u>. London: Oxford University Press.

Boxil, E. H. (1985). <u>Music therapy for the developmentally disabled</u>. Maryland: Aspen Systems Corporation.

Foxx, R. M. (1982). <u>Decreasing Behaviors of Persons with Severe Retardation and Autism</u>. Champaign, IL: Research Press.

Lovaas, O. I. (1987). Behavioral treatment and normal educational and intellectual functioning in young autistic children. <u>Journal of Consulting and Clinical Psychology</u>, <u>55</u>, 3-9.

Newman, B. (1999). <u>When Everybody Cares: Case Studies of ABA with People with Autism</u>. New York; Dove and Orca.

PECS

Pyramid Educational Consultants, Inc.

226 West Park Place, Suite 1

Newark, Delaware 19711

1-888-PECS INC (732-7462)

www.pecs.com

PICTURE THIS

SilverLining Multimedia, Inc.

PO Box 2201

Poughkeepsie, New York 12601

914-462-8714

These products and more can be ordered, very conveniently, from: DIFFERENT ROADS TO LEARNING, INC., a catalog of useful products.   1-800-853-1057   www.difflearn.com

Suggested Readings

Bailey, J. S. (1991). Promoting freedom and dignity: A new agenda for behavior analysis. Paper presented at the annual convention of the Association for Behavior Analysis, May 1991.

Bijou, S. W. (1970). What psychology has to offer education- now. Journal of Applied Behavior Analysis, 3, 65-71.

Binder, C., & Watkins, C.L. (1989). Promoting effective instructional methods: Solutions to America's educational crisis. Future Choices, 1(3), 33-39.

Carr, E. G., & Durand, V. M. (1985). Reducing behavior problems through functional communication training. Journal of Applied Behavior Analysis, 18, 111-126.

Cooper, J.O., Heron, T.E., & Heward, W.L. (1987). Applied behavior analysis. Toronto: Merrill Publishing.

Foxx, R. M. (1982). Increasing behavior of persons with severe retardation and autism. Champaign,IL: Research Press.

Goetz, E.M. & Baer, D. M. (1974). Social control of form diversity and the emergence of new forms in children's blockbuilding. Journal of Applied Behavior Analysis, 6, 209-217.

Lovaas, O. I. (1987). Behavioral treatment and normal educational and intellectual functioning in young autistic children. Journal of Consulting and Clinical Psychology, 55, 3-9.

Lovaas, O. I. (1981). Teaching developmentally disabled children: The ME book. Austin: Pro-Ed.

Malott, R. W. (1989). The achievement of evasive goals: Control by rules describing contingencies that are not direct acting. In S.C. Hayes (Ed.) Rule-governed behavior: Cognition, contingencies and instructional control (pp. 269-322). New York: Plenum Press.

Maurice, C., Green, G., & Luce, S. C. (Eds.) Behavioral Intervention for Young Children with Autism. Austin: Pro-Ed.

Newman, B. (1992). The reluctant alliance: Behaviorism and humanism. Buffalo, NY: Prometheus Books.

Sidman, M. (1989). Coercion and its fallout. Boston: Authors Cooperative.

Skinner, B. F. (1953). <u>Science and human behavior</u>. New York: The Free Press.

Skinner, B. F. (1971). Humanistic behaviorism. <u>The Humanist</u>, <u>31</u>(3), 35.

Skinner, B. F. (1972). Humanism and behaviorism. <u>The Humanist</u>, <u>32</u>(4), 18-20.

Skinner, B. F. (1976). The ethics of helping people. <u>The Humanist</u>, <u>36</u>(1), 7-11.

Van Houten, R., Axelrod, S., Bailey, J. S., Favell, J. E., Foxx, R. M., Iwata, B. A., & Lovaas, O. I. (1988). The right to effective behavioral treatment. <u>Journal of Applied Behavior Analysis</u>, <u>21</u>, 381-384.

Made in the USA
Columbia, SC
13 September 2018